D0637832

A CALL TO WORSHIP

A CALL TO WORSHIP

Randy T. Hodges

Beacon Hill Press of Kansas City
Kansas City, Missouri

Copyright 1996
by Beacon Hill Press of Kansas City

ISBN 083-411-5778

Printed in the
United States of America

Cover Design: Mike Walsh

Library of Congress Cataloging-in-Publication Data
Hodges, Randy T., 1955-
    A call to worship / Randy T. Hodges.
    157 p. 21 cm.
    Includes bibliographical references.
    ISBN 0-8341-1577-8 (pb)
    1. Public worship. I. Title
  BV15.H64   1996
  264—dc20

96-2576
CIP

10 9 8 7 6 5 4 3 2 1

To Michelle, Adam, and Denise,
in whose loving support I sense God's goodness

CONTENTS

FOREWORD

One of the most heartening signs of the times is the Holy Spirit's reawakening of the Church to its primary duty in worship. Evangelical churches everywhere are showing a fresh interest in the subject. Accompanying this revival is widespread confusion as to what really constitutes worship. One of the big concerns is this question: Should the Church abandon its time-tested forms of worship in order to reach those who are turned off by these "traditional" forms and are demanding more "contemporary" music and worship styles?

Randy Hodges addresses this controversial subject. Writing as a seasoned pastor, he has thoroughly researched this topic. From the perspective of a scholar he provides the theoretical basis for worship. From the perspective of a field researcher, one who has visited many churches of varying sizes and different denominations, he describes and analyzes worship practices. This field research has been further extended as Dr. Hodges and his congregation have incorporated the principles of this book in order to evangelize their community.

Hodges begins by making a convincing case for the Church's being a worshiping community. He does this by distinguishing worship from entertainment, evangelism, and other practices that sometimes pass for worship. Worship, Hodges argues, is an end in itself, and every other phase of the Church's life must contribute to the worship of God.

The early chapters lay a theological foundation for the author's thesis. Although Hodges writes from the Wesleyan-Holiness presupposition that the Christian life is one of victory over sin, his treatment of worship reflects classical Christian understandings that transcend denominational emphases. For example, he follows John Wesley in including confession of sin in public worship as a means of fostering growth in holiness. Especially helpful is his illuminating depiction of "the flow of good worship" in the second chapter. The theological presupposition that worship is the primary duty of the Church controls the practical discussions that follow.

In his discussion of the traditional-contemporary controversy he literally "faces the music" and takes a mediating position on this hot topic. He takes the reader on a tour of some of the "great" churches today that are experimenting with newer forms of worship and assesses what he sees as their strengths and weaknesses. At the same time he is aware that most of his readers will be serving congregations that are comparatively small. He cautions against abruptly breaking worship and music traditions and offers guidance for making positive changes without disrupting the life of the church.

As I read this timely book I was impressed by the sanity and spiritual sensitivity with which Dr. Hodges handles the tough questions that are bound to arise when an urban church comes to grips with the challenge of providing meaningful worship for the people of God while sensitizing and adjusting itself to the needs of modern pagans beginning to show religious interest. I have witnessed for myself how he and his people are successfully putting into practice what he proposes in these pages.

Whatever the size of your congregation, Hodges has written with you in mind. His study has meaning for churches of all sizes. While he now pastors a growing, middle-sized church, this study was underway when he was pastor of smaller congregations.

I heartily recommend this book to you, whether you are a beginning or seasoned pastor. In its pages, I am confident, you will find stimulus, guidance, and inspiration for the work to which God has called you.

—William M. Greathouse
General Superintendent Emeritus
Church of the Nazarene

ACKNOWLEDGMENTS

God uses many positive influences to complete anything worthwhile, and this book is no exception. I must express my appreciation to those who have positively touched me:

- To the congregations who have called me "pastor," especially the folks of West Side Church of the Nazarene in Wichita, Kansas, whose consistent encouragement and support have made me a better person as we labor *"Together . . . Winning the Lost, Building the Found."*

- To Barbara McKee, my secretary, who efficiently stays on top of so many details and keeps at least two steps ahead of me.

- To Jack Rennie, whose consistent love for God and people has enabled him to lead the music ministry of West Side Church of the Nazarene for more than two and a half decades.

- To Rolf Kleinfeld, whose often zany enthusiasm kept us smiling.

- To Albert Truesdale, whose persistence taught me to be a better writer (even when I resisted!).

- To William Greathouse, whom God has used to encourage, guide, and prompt me so many times in my life as a minister.

- And most importantly, to my wife and children, Michelle, Adam, and Denise, whose love makes life a delightful adventure.

Thanks for your love, support, and encouragement! You're all great!

1

Worship—the Church's First Priority

What's Really Important?

THE CHURCH—SO MUCH TO DO, SO MUCH EXPECT-ed, such meager earthly resources to get it all done. Who else understands their mission as reaching the whole world while attempting to minister to persons from the womb to the tomb? If you've spent much time pastoring a congregation, you've probably felt like the guy who had a sign behind his desk that read, "We've done so much for so long with so little that we are now qualified to do anything with absolutely nothing."

A multitude of expectations exist for the church in our consumer-oriented society. The demand seems ever-growing. Some megachurches rush to meet the varied expectations. A resource guide offered to first-time visitors of a "hugely successful," well-known Midwestern congregation lists among its ministry offerings such specialized and diverse programs as Alone and Pregnant, Dads' Ministry, Moms' Ministry, Father-Daughter Camp, Father-Son Camp, Inner-city Ministry, and International Ministry. To this list add a plethora of self-help groups, including AA, ACOA, Al-Anon, Al-Kids, CodA, S-Anon, Al-teen, DA, EA, NA, OA, SA, and ISA. (Quite an "alphabet soup" of self-help groups! They attempt to minister to the increasing number of felt needs driving our consumer-oriented society.

Besides this sampling of ministries, a resource guide for this congregation lists *an additional 84 specialized ministries* designed to "scratch the needs where people now itch." In the same church a full-service bookstore is open daily to offer Christian reading materials and tapes. People can browse to find what they need after any of the church's services, which are conveniently offered Wednesdays, Thursdays, Saturdays, and Sundays. Or after services worshipers may choose to have fellowship and build community in the "food court," just like in the mall, where a host of eating options are available. Among other options, there's a salad bar for the weight-conscious and an ice-cream stand for the others. If a person overindulges on the banana split, he or she can move to the sports and fitness center to burn off that unsightly waistline.

Am I throwing stones at this diverse smorgasbord of ministry options? Not at all. The array of offerings is cited only to show how our world expects *so much* from the church—perhaps unrealistically so. I suspect those responsible for supervising the programming of this congregation could easily grow weary just reading the latest batch of suggestions for new ministries their church ought to be providing. Our consumer-oriented society expects a lot from the church.

Most of us lead congregations with more limited resources. Many pastors work solo. As the sole staff in our place of service, even a part-time secretary would be a delightful help. Others may have some secretarial or staff assistance. But whether large- or small-church pastors, most can identify the hurts and needs of the people surrounding them. The wounds and pain are all too easy to spot. Most pastors make a valiant effort to do what they can. But the reality is that limited time, limited energy, limited staff, and limited budget mean we never catch up with the demand. While God is all-powerful, is any place He needs to be, and owns "the cattle on a thousand hills" (Ps. 50:10), we do not. We work with limited resources in a society with insatiable demands. Simply to survive, we have to do what is most important.

What *is* really important? If the church was to do only one thing and nothing else, what would that be?

The central thesis of this book is that *the most important activity in any church is worshiping God in His holiness.* Glorifying and honoring God through worship is the primary and essential activity of the Church of Jesus Christ. The very life of the Church flows from its worship. With Jesus as the head, worship is the heart of the Body of Christ.

This is no new revelation. "The primary work of the church is worship," says worship renewal advocate Robert Webber. "Indeed, I have discovered in my own life that corporate worship is the taproot of my life. It is the source of spiritual life and growth."[1] Webber goes on to emphasize his point, that worship is the hub around which the Church revolves, by citing the liturgical constitution of Vatican II: "The liturgy (worship) is the summit toward which the activity of the church is directed; at the same time it is a fount from which all the church's power flows."[2]

Anne Ortlund has written a wonderful book she calls *Up with Worship.* Even her title suggests the primacy of worship in the life of the Church. She says more explicitly, "A Christian must arrange his schedule around the weekly worship service. No Bible classes or missionary committee meetings must interfere. Worshiping churches will make sure that every member worships—and will insist that they do for the health of the Body. The total church program must revolve around that holy hour!"[3]

Another church leader confronts pastors with the centrality of worship:

> I am convinced that nothing we do as Christ's ministers is more important than our personal worship and our conduct

of public worship, in which we have the high privilege of leading God's people into a living encounter with Him in His holiness and His grace . . . True worship, I am convinced, is the vital spark of heavenly flame that inspires, refines, sustains, and builds up the life of the church. Worship is the highest act of which a creature of God is capable.[4]

If the Church does only one thing, it must worship. The essential and primary activity of the Church is worshiping God in His holiness.

What Is Worship?

Since worshiping God in His holiness is the essential activity of the Church, we must clearly understand what worship is. "There seems to be in many churches confusion as to what really constitutes worship," observes one denominational leader.[5] He continues, "Of course, this is nothing new. More than 40 years ago General Superintendent Chapman complained that many of our services had more of the atmosphere of 'an old-fashioned mountain corn husking' than of the worship of almighty God."[6] Obviously, worship is a continuing concern. Let's briefly explore the nature of true worship by first understanding what corporate worship is not.

Worship is not entertainment—although when we worship God rightly there should be no activity that satisfies and fulfills us more thoroughly. Since music is so central to Christian worship, it is also a key area in which there is danger of delivering worship over to the "god of entertainment." James Spruce cautions us that it is in Christian music "where the blending of sacred and secular music is so subtly done that the differences between Christian praise and worldly entertainment are often confused if not indistinguishable. The response of the passive worshiper is often failure to distinguish between what is truly entertaining and what is truly God-honoring."[7]

Occasionally it is easy to distinguish music delivered as performance from that offered as worship. The response of one congregation to the singer at a Lord's day morning service showed they knew entertainment when they saw it. This congregation commonly responded to those who sang in the services with "Amen" or "Praise the Lord." But to this obvious performance the congregation simply broke into applause. Their common worship patterns were abandoned, for they instinctively perceived they were experiencing not ministry but entertainment. The focus left God, and they immediately went to the world's method of expressing approval of entertainers. This was so uncharacteristic for this congregation that it was obvious they were clapping for the performer-entertainer rather than praising the God on whom worship is supposed to focus. While applause may not always indicate an "entertainment mind-set," in this situation the congregational response clearly indicated their assessment of what was happening.

Dennis Crocker helps us see why the trend of turning worship services into entertainment spectaculars seems so prevalent. "I fear we have been conditioned by the pervasive influence of television to *expect* to be entertained," he writes. "This expectation is intensified in many instances by religious TV programs in which entertainment plays a major role. We passively sit and watch television; and when we come to church, we may have the same expectations."[8]

This is not an argument to justify boring worship services. Worship should never be allowed to degenerate to the level of boring monotony. The option is not entertainment or uninspired dullness. But perhaps the greatest danger we face from falling into the "We've got to entertain them" mode is that it removes the focus from God, placing it either on the audience (who are not really worshipers) or upon the performers (who are not really worship leaders). When either of these becomes the focus of what we are doing, we have moved away from genuine worship. Real worship focuses on God.

It is frightening that in many places worship has thoroughly embraced our culture's fixation on entertainment.

While there are those who argue that "we have to entertain them to attract or hold them," we should fear a far worse outcome. In forsaking the church's primary calling (that is, *worship*), people will soon instinctively realize something is wrong. When they come to this conclusion, they will leave anyway. Entertainment is to worship what fast food is to a healthful diet. It may please in the short run, but when we partake too often, we discover we long for something more substantial, something more satisfying. Maturing Christians cannot grow from a steady diet of entertainment. Worship is not entertainment.

Worship is not evangelism—although people will be saved as the church glorifies God and the gospel is faithfully proclaimed. In my formative years growing up in the church, I concluded the most important thing any believer can do is to share Christ with those who are lost. I have talked with others who believed likewise. Over time, however, I have come to see that behind evangelism lies the even more important work of worship. If we worship God rightly, the outcome will be a more serious and intense commitment to do the will and work of God, which certainly includes taking the gospel to the lost. Yet it is not difficult to understand why some of us have come to believe that the reason we come together in worship is to make converts.

A look at our roots offers insight into why many of us view worship as an opportunity to evangelize. John Wesley, the father of Methodism and a spiritual forefather of many denominations, faced a dilemma: How could he reach the unchurched masses in the new industrial and mining centers of England? His answer was to develop a new type of meeting that focused on making converts. Field preaching, taking the gospel to the lost, became his effective strategy and caused many to turn to Christ. But Wesley, a committed Anglican churchman, was not attempting to subvert worship. Rather, he was searching for an effective way to take the gospel to those who needed Christ. In finding the answer to the problem he faced, it just happened that the worship patterns of the church were altered. Wesley found himself out of favor with the Anglican Church, and Methodism was launched. Early Methodist worship thus came into being with a heart burning for evangelism. With our roots having such an intense interest in saving the lost, it would be amazing if we did not place a high priority on evangelism.

In addition to Methodism, worship has been influenced by the "frontier-revival tradition." Churches influenced by this tradition acquired distinctive characteristics that came as a result of the American frontier. This included any American church group that arose after the 1820s. Key characteristics of frontier worship included pragmatism (doing what works), the camp meeting, a passion for making converts through evangelistic preaching, and an emphasis on congregational singing. Perhaps the key trait of frontier worship was that worship "was specifically designed to make converts."[9]

At first there was a clear understanding of the difference between services of worship and services of evangelism. "It was never the intention of the leaders," says worship historian and advocate Robert Webber, "that these revival services replace the worship of the church. However, the revival approach was gradually assimilated by the church and here and there replaced Sunday morning worship."[10] A subtle and gradual change took place in worship that shifted the focus of the service from glorifying God to converting those needing to find salvation.

John R. Stott says of those of us who call ourselves evangelicals, "We evangelicals do not know much about worship. Evangelism is our specialty, not worship. We have little sense of the greatness of almighty God."[11] The point of this discussion *is not* to devalue evangelism. A church that is alive with the Spirit of God *will* be an outreaching, soul-winning church. The point is that our tradition has most often placed such emphasis on evangelism that we have sometimes forgotten the primacy of worshiping God.

Two ironies present themselves relating to this emphasis on evangelism in worship. One is that in an atmosphere where worship is designed primarily to evangelize, we can create persons who, once they are saved, believe their role is simply to "show up, pay up, and shut up." An "I've already done that" attitude can develop in believers who attend services—an attitude that creates passive spectators rather than active participants in worship. God deserves better.

A second irony involves congregational expectations when people are trained that worship is evangelism. Even though the pastor may be preaching only to those who have faithfully attended the same church for decades, there can be an uneasiness in some worshipers if not every sermon and service ends in an evangelistic invitation. While evangelistic invitations ought to be frequent, the Holy Spirit also wishes to speak to and challenge those already committed to advance in their faith. Evangelism will naturally flow from services of worship, but worship is not merely evangelism.

Worship is not promotion of the church's programs—although during services of worship, persons may be made aware of other opportunities for ministering and being ministered to in the Body of Christ. It is possible in this age of specialization to focus upon valid and important ministries of the church so much that they are substituted for real worship. We can parade one group or cause after another before our people almost as if we pride ourselves in how much activity is occurring in our congregation. In the name of sharing with the larger congregation what is happening in the many ministries of the church, we can focus one week on children's ministries, another on teen quizzing, and yet another on the junior choir. These specialized activities can be followed by centering our attention on youth retreats, fundraisers, lock-ins, and outreaches. We can follow up by focusing on singles retreats and then on senior adult activities that can be just as diverse. Ladies' ministries, men's ministries, marriage enrichment ministries, and a host of other important activities can easily squeeze God out of His rightful place in the center of the spotlight of worship.

Worship begins and ends with God. While these activities and specialized ministries are important, they can subtly move the focus of our worship away from our holy God. In focusing on one or more of the various ministries, we can miss true worship. To put the church's ministries in the place rightly belonging to God is to engage in a subtle but hideous idolatry.

Worship is not fund-raising—although giving is a natural expression of believers who seek to be like our gracious and generous God. You've probably had conversations like one I had recently with someone from my church. She told me of a nearby church where several people were leaving because "All the preacher talks about is money." Whether this pastor was guilty of overemphasizing financial matters or not, the perception of some became that the church was primarily a money-collecting organization.

Others so strongly fear negative reaction from members of their congregation that they choose to eliminate all public mention of finances. While visiting a large congregation with nearly 1,500 persons present at the 8 A.M. early service, I was struck by their not passing offering plates during the service. In the "visitor brochure" I found the explanation:

> One of the long-standing traditions of [this church] is to not pass an offering plate during our services. When you want to share in the ministry financially, you can put your tax-deductible gift in one of the offering boxes located at each exit of the sanctuary, or simply mail your gift to the church office.

Both of these cases illustrate extremes that suggest a need for balance in training congregations in matters of Christ-honoring stewardship. It has been my personal experience in pastoring four churches that by "sticking to the business" of worship, congregational giving has increased to levels not previously attained by those congregations. It is not that I have refused to talk about the importance of giving. Nor have I kept the ushers from passing the offering plates. But by setting the offering in the context of worship, people have responded generously.

It is typical for me to tell the congregation before the offering that "Christians are generous people, because our Lord is a generous God." Or, "When we worship God, we commit our whole selves to Him. Every aspect of our lives is surrendered to Him in worship, including our finances. So today we present to Him His tithes and our offerings."

This agrees with what Paul said of the early Macedonian church, regarding their surprising generosity: "And they did not do as we expected, but they gave themselves first to the Lord and then to us in keeping with God's will" (2 Cor. 8:5).[12] When financial stewardship is placed in the context of worship, people even look forward to sermons focusing on biblical stewardship. This is a very different approach than coming to the time of offering with the ominous words "Folks, the church is in desperate financial need again this week." Worship is something other than fund-raising.

Several other things worship is not. Many legitimate and necessary activities occur in the church that are not worship. Without belaboring what worship is not, let me simply mention a few items that may help us to better understand the nature of genuine worship. In addition to those items already identified that are not worship, we might add **fellowship**—although when the family of God comes together, there should be a joyous unity and oneness that is special and precious. Anne Ortlund writes, "Some churches become fellowship centers—evangelical Kiwanis Clubs ('the more we get together, the happier we'll be')."[13] While fellowship is an important part of life in the body, fellowship is not worship.

Worship is also not **church growth**—although when the people of God come together to lift up Christ, the Lord himself has said, "I will build my church, and the gates of Hades will not overcome it" (Matt. 16:18).

Worship is also not **education**—although when God's people join to praise Him, there will be new and glorious insights as the Spirit leads us into all truth. In eliminating these many things that worship is not, we come to see more clearly one truth: **Worship is an end in itself—to worship is to glorify God.**

The only legitimate focus of worship is God himself. God declares, "I am the LORD; that is my name! I will not give my glory to another or my praise to idols" (Isa. 42:8). It is too easy for the *functions* of church life to become the *focus* of the church. Machinery becomes the end. Activity substitutes for real life. Busyness becomes the pattern that quickly justifies itself, and we don't even discern that God has departed from our midst. When God is dethroned and we idolatrously worship the programs we have created rather than the Creator himself, our church dies.

But when God remains the central focus, when we come together for the sole purpose of glorifying Him, all the other activities assume their rightful places. The pieces fit when God is worshiped. When the body assembles to worship Him—to praise, glorify, and exalt Him in His majesty, to love the Holy One of Israel—we put first things first. It is the Westminster catechism that teaches us that "the chief end of man is to glorify God and enjoy Him forever." Likewise, the primary and essential activity of the Church is to glorify God.

In a day when the question "What's in it for me?" quickly rolls through our minds, William Greathouse reminds us, "We do not go to worship for what we can get, but rather what we can give, to give glory to God, to honor Him, magnify and bless His name. There is a correct 'getting' dimension to worship. We do not worship to be entertained or even educated, but we can engage in no activity more fulfilling or edifying or more thrilling than that of true worship."[14]

In worship, those called to be elders in the church help present God to the people and the people to God—

this is the central activity of ministry and the fountainhead of all else that the church does and is. Ralph P. Martin says worship is the "dramatic celebration of God in His supreme worth in such a manner that His 'worthiness' becomes the norm and inspiration of human living."[15] Worship is the prime activity of the church, in which we glorify God. It is the regularly scheduled meeting in which we declare and redeclare our love to God. It is the opportunity for those of us who call ourselves "Christ's ones" to stand and proclaim, "We love You, Father."

The Purpose and Plan

It is obvious by now that this book is about worship—to be more specific, corporate worship: God's people coming together in Christ Jesus *for the sole purpose of glorifying God.* Written primarily to pastors and those eager to know more about worship, this book is a resource to guide and enlarge our understanding of Christian corporate worship and to equip us to lead more effectively.

The following chapters will discuss many issues. We will ask, "What's to happen when we worship?" We will dive into the debate on seeker-sensitive worship as we ask, "Who is worship for?" And since the Church worships in the midst of the surrounding culture, we will examine what is happening around us, and then we will explore some implications contemporary culture may have for the way we shape and conduct services of worship. We will try to handle the hot potato of competing worship styles as we face the music. Will it be anthems, hymns, or choruses for you? In a closing section, suggestions will be offered for expanding our vision of what worship can and should be, as well as how we can assess our congregation's present patterns of worship. Finally, in a chapter with the alternate title "How to Make Worship Changes Without Changing Churches," we will examine how to responsibly effect positive change in worship.

Who Shapes the Services of Worship?

Worship is the work of the people. A quick look at the dictionary reveals that "liturgy," a word describing the public worship of the church, is comprised from two Greek words—*laos* (people) and *ergon* (work). From the earliest days, even the words used to describe the public worship of the Body of Christ recognized that glorifying God is the business of the whole body, not just the clergy. Worship is the work of *the people*. Without their active involvement, worship has not taken place. For this reason, it is vital that we remember that worship depends on more than the personal preferences of the pastor. It is unwise for the pastor to so dominate decisions about the services of worship that the feelings, preferences, and patterns to which the people are accustomed are disregarded or ignored. Those in the pews can be left feeling abandoned.

Today changes in worship patterns have occurred rapidly, particularly with the arrival of what is often labeled "contemporary worship." While new patterns may speak more effectively to our surrounding culture, it is also essential that we not forsake those who have been trained in our own congregation's past patterns and styles of worship. To persons who have come to Christ and who have worshiped in our services for decades, these patterns have become their gateway into the presence of God. These folks who have been saved at our altars and raised up in our worship services are persons to and for whom we are responsible. We must not move to "new" and different styles without also providing for their spiritual care and feeding.

Having shared this word of caution (which we will discuss more fully in chapter 6), let us understand that more than any other person, the pastor shapes, guides, and influences the services of worship. Thomas Oden, in his masterful *Pastoral Theology* writes,

> One of the strongest forces in pastoral identity is the public role of leader of the worshiping community. However

diverse their other social roles, pastors are publicly identified most often as leaders of worship. Wherever they go, people characteristically think of them in relation to this distinctive public task and context. Thus, even if one's central interests may lie elsewhere, one is well advised to understand this expectation clearly and then carefully examine one's own attitudes about it.[16]

Oden calls the pastor "the chief, but not the sole liturgist."[17] As we've seen, the word "liturgy" points to the truth that worship is the work of the people. "Liturgy" is not a word we need to fear or shun, although we probably feel less comfortable with it than some other sectors of Christianity. Simply understood, liturgy can be thought of as our order of service, or perhaps as how we "do worship." Oden goes on to speak of the pastor's central role in shaping worship by saying, "As liturgical leader of the congregation, the pastor is responsible for organizing, interpreting, and presiding over the whole arena of worship, usually in consultation with laity through a church commission on worship."[18]

Since the pastor's role in shaping the services of worship is so influential, we who lead carry a heavy responsibility. We must know what should happen when we worship. This issue is the central concern of our next chapter.

2

What's to Happen When We Worship?

SHE WAS NOT A NEWCOMER TO WORSHIP SERVICES. Dorothy grew up in a Christian home. She and her husband raised their children in church services. She had sat through literally thousands of church services, and her demeanor suggested she probably enjoyed and supported almost every one of them. For many of those services, she masterfully played the organ with skill and spiritual sensitivity. A respected and insightful leader in the church, Dorothy's committed service to the Lord made her words especially thought-provoking: "Pastor, I have never before stopped to consider what is supposed to happen when we worship."

I'm glad she said those words to me. For the first time I realized that if reflective, spiritually minded believers like Dorothy have never seriously considered what's to happen when we worship, then there are many others just like her. For that matter, how many of us who are charged with the responsibility of planning and leading worship have seriously considered what's supposed to happen when God's people gather to worship?

Thomas Oden, in *Pastoral Theology*, calls us to account as he writes, "The public worship that the pastor leads must itself be clearly understood by the pastor."[1] While his statement seems obvious, we know how many services are planned. We flip through the hymnal to find two congregational hymns. A baby dedication must fit into the order of service. We need a slot to insert the choir arrangement, the offering, the sermon, certainly an invitation, and maybe, if there's time, a spot for testimonies. Oh, yes—Tom's sister is visiting from Houston. He asked if she could sing a special. She'll sing just before the sermon. Announcements never seem to fit, but eventually we stick them just before the offering. We piece together the individual components of next Sunday's service like assembling a jigsaw puzzle without the box-top picture to follow. Most often we end up doing this week's service just like we did last week's.

Is there more to planning an effective service of worship than making sure we use all the pieces? Is it possible that good worship could have a "flow" to it that intentionally leads worshipers closer to God? Could it be that God has supplied us with the "box-top picture" to guide us in worship planning? Where should worship start, and, perhaps more important, where should it seek to end as we lead God's people? What is supposed to happen when we worship?

Worship Planning—Opening the Doors to God's Movement

Let's be quick to understand that knowing what should happen in worship is not to restrict or rule out God's spontaneous movement in our services. We must guard against so structuring our worship services that God himself cannot get in. William H. Willimon, in his book *Worship as Pastoral Care*, talks about two traps into which worship leaders can fall: We can subconsciously demand to be in control so much that we unwittingly stifle God's attempts to move in our midst—or, Willimon suggests, it is possible that some worship leaders can so desire to be the center of attention that they refuse to yield the spotlight to God. Rather than being a vehicle through which God works, these leaders wrongly place themselves at center stage with no plans to step aside for God.² If these problems of relinquishing control or needing attention are ours, attempts to structure worship will not be effective. The refusal to give first place to God reveals a problem in our own relationship with Him.

We must recognize that there is nothing more spiritually satisfying than having God move into our midst and transform the elements of worship—the special music, the Scripture, or even the words of the sermon—into life-changing vehicles. Simply put, worship leaders must let God be God!

Do you remember what happened when Solomon finished constructing the Temple? Building a permanent house of worship for God to replace the Tabernacle had been a dream that was denied to Solomon's father, David. But now, many years and much work later, the Temple was finally ready. At the "grand opening," all the men of Israel were called together. Many exciting events were planned in the worship to honor and magnify God. The highlight of the dedication would be placing the ark of the covenant, the symbol of God's presence, into the holy of holies.

When the priests delivered the ark to its new home, a most amazing thing happened. The Scripture says it like this, "When the priests withdrew from the Holy Place, the cloud filled the temple of the LORD. And the priests could not perform their service because of the cloud, for the glory of the LORD filled his temple" (1 Kings 8:10-11). The visible glory of God fell so powerfully on that celebration of worship that the priests had no choice but to step aside and gaze in awe on God's holy splendor.

Oh, that there will be times when God's glory falls on our services of worship! We need those blessed occasions when we who fill the priestly role of worship leader simply stand back and let God reveal himself again. We need Him in our services today. But notice that when God descended in His glory at the dedication of the Temple, it was not because the worship was ill-prepared. It was not because the priests had nothing else ready. The details of that worship event had been carefully planned. Yet God, in His sovereign timing, knew just when and how to change the planned order of service to something much better. Of course, not even Solomon or his priests could orchestrate the inbreaking of the glory of God. Their effective worship planning, or ours, does not eliminate or restrict God's movement in our midst. Rather, by taking seriously what is supposed to happen when we worship together, careful and informed planning actually opens the door for God to enter more easily.

How can we lead our congregation in a manner that will let them know God's plans take precedence? Since our people need to be routinely reminded that God's plans are most important, we place below the order of service this brief sentence: *"The order of service is subject to change by the direction of the Holy Spirit."* Joined with a sensitivity to what God is doing, our people will become aware that God indeed is the focus of worship.

Where Do We Get Our Cues for Good Worship?

Before we consider what's to happen in good worship, it is important to ask, "Where do we get our worship cues?" Let's admit it. We are heavily influenced by the entertainment industry. The graphic images that enter our minds by way of the airwaves leave memorable impressions that are hard to forget. Could it be that some of us, perhaps unwittingly, take our cues for worship from what we see on television?

A minister of music, advocating that we start each service with the same chorus, reasoned with me in this way: "Pastor, we need a theme song to begin our service—just like they use on television programs." Whether or not using a "theme song" to begin each service is a good idea is not the issue. But a real problem exists if the worship of Almighty God is shaped largely by the glitz and shallowness of what we see in the entertainment industry. William Greathouse in "The Present Crisis in Our Worship" states,

> Worship is not something done before or for the congregation, as if those leading the services are the actors and the congregation the audience. No, but as Søren Kierkegaard reminds us, in Christian worship the worship leaders are simply "prompters," for the true "actors" are the people of God gathered to ascribe worth, honor, and praise to almighty God. The "performance" is not by the leaders but by the congregation. George Frideric Handel's classic statement in 1741 after the premiere of his *Messiah* is still valid: "Sir, I should be sorry if I only entertained them. I had hoped it would make them better."[3]

Another common source shaping how we do worship finds its roots in pragmatism—that is, finding what works and then copying it. We search out "successful churches," use the criteria of size or growth as our measuring stick, and then borrow their patterns as our model. There may be merit in examining what God blesses in other situations, but we need better criteria to guide what we should and should not do in worship than just asking "What's working elsewhere?" Blindly copying the patterns of others could unexpectedly lead us where we don't want to go.

In January 1982 the precision flying team of the United States Air Force, the Thunderbirds, suffered a horrible accident. While the Thunderbird jets thrill millions of spectators each year with their daring and precise maneuvers, this day turned deadly. During a practice session, while traveling more than 400 miles per hour, within milliseconds all four jets crashed into the desert ground. Four pilots died instantly.

What had happened? A spokesperson for the Air Force speculated it may well have been a case of "follow the leader into the ground." "The Thunderbird pilots are trained to 'fly off the commander-leader,' watching only the plane next to them and not the ground or their instruments because of the tight formation in which they fly—often as close as three feet apart," he explained. "Normally the commander-leader is the only one looking where he's going," the spokesperson said.[4]

"Follow the leader into the ground." What a tragic end to the lives of four young, healthy pilots! Would it not be equally tragic if we in worship blindly followed some supposed leader to destruction because the leader (or we) did not really know where he or she was going? We must have a more reliable guide to good worship than merely asking, "What works?" and then imitating what we see.

Obviously other factors shape our worship. Tradition shapes what happens when we worship. So do the personal preferences and personality of the worship leader. What music support is available is another key factor that determines what can and can't be done in services of worship.

While these factors, and many others, influence what happens when we unite to worship God, ultimately the one reliable source that must guide our worship planning is the Word of God. Patterns to effective worship are revealed in the holy Scriptures. They will guide us in knowing what is supposed to happen in worship if we listen. These basic patterns of good worship provide for us safe and authoritative guidelines that let us know what is and is not acceptable. They serve a role similar to the black lines painted around the perimeter of a basketball court. Because the lines are clearly marked, the players and officials can easily see what is inbounds and what is out. Likewise, the patterns of worship revealed in God's Word give God's worship leaders clear direction in acceptable, God-pleasing worship. Let's examine some of the major patterns of biblical worship.

Good Worship Has a Sense of "Flow"

Understanding the flow of good worship is foundational. Having in mind a sense of where worship begins, what touchstones to pass, and what destination to pursue serves to guide right thinking and planning of services. "An ideal service of worship: (1) will bring the people into an awareness and realization of God's awesome, glorious, and beautiful holiness; (2) which will in turn elicit a confession of need that opens hearts and lives to the healing and cleansing presence of God; and (3) issues in them a glad yielding up of their beings to the service and purpose of God in their everyday world."[5] Respected Wesleyan scholar Thomas Oden echoes this thought: "Christian worship proceeds from awe through pardon to dedication."[6] This flow in good worship is not merely a personal insight of a few selected individuals, but it is also Scripture-based. Comprehending the flow of good worship is a matter of seeing more clearly what God reveals in His holy Word.

Patterns of Good Worship

At least five patterns or "movements" of good worship are outlined in the Bible. These patterns provide us with a framework on which we can build our plans for services of worship and responsibly lead our people to worship Almighty God.

Good worship begins by focusing on God in *praise and adoration.*

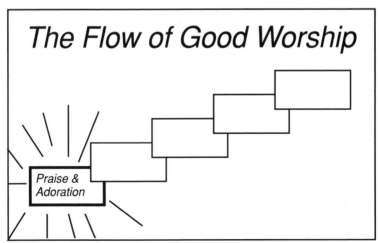

The Flow of Good Worship

Praise & Adoration

A Good Beginning

"Give me a place to stand, and I will move the earth," declared Archimedes. He knew a solid foundation would enable great things to follow. The solid foundation for good worship is *adoration and praise*. Adoration and praise are our proper responses to a holy God. In adoration we praise God for who He is, the Holy One of Israel. The Old Testament prophet Isaiah paints a beautiful word picture of how real worship should start. Hear his "call to worship":

> Give thanks to the LORD, call on his name; make known among the nations what he has done, and proclaim that his name is exalted. Sing to the LORD, for he has done glorious things; let this be known to all the world. Shout aloud and sing for joy, people of Zion, for great is the Holy One of Israel among you *(Isa. 12:4-6)*.

In adoration we exalt and lift God up—for His holiness and for what He has done. By beginning the service of worship by focusing on God, we lay a solid foundation for great things to follow. Psalm 103 guides us in seeing the breadth of our praise as we worship God first for His holiness and then for the blessings He gives: "Praise the LORD, O my soul; all my inmost being, praise his holy name. Praise the LORD, O my soul, and forget not all his benefits" (Ps. 103:1-2).

Praising God for His Holiness

When we approach God in adoration and praise, it is important that we lift up His holiness. While most people today are not naturally comfortable with the idea of holiness, worship should cause us to realize that God is not just "the man upstairs" or "our heavenly good buddy." Worship must instruct people in the meaning of God's holiness. A chatty familiarity with God is based not on intimacy but on disrespect and blindness to who God is—the Holy One. In focusing on God's holiness, we acknowledge and teach that He is separate from and totally above us. God is totally and unmistakably superior. Unless we present God as holy, those we lead in worship will never stand in awe and reverence before Him.

H. Ray Dunning observes, "Holiness is that essential character of Deity that places God in a completely exclusive category and sharply distinguishes Him from the human and the naturalistic. . . . His holiness gives God the right to claim undivided or unshared love and worship."[7] Because of God's holiness, majesty, and splendor, awe and reverence are our only right responses. Robert Webber observes, "If Christ came physically, and actually stood in the midst of a people at worship . . . we would probably kneel, maybe even fall prostrate before him."[8] Our natural response, if we really see God's holiness, is to bow in reverent adoration before Him.

A Biblical Model Focusing on God's Holiness

Isaiah's vision in the Temple illustrates how seeing God in His holiness serves as the foundation for good worship. The seraphs called to one another, "Holy, holy, holy is the LORD Almighty; the whole earth is full of his glory" (Isa. 6:3). The Hebrew language emphasizes God's holiness by repeating the word "holy." In North American English we would probably say, "The Lord is very, very holy."[9] Isaiah's vision, recognized by many biblical and worship scholars as the foremost scriptural pattern for worship, begins by emphasizing praise and adoration of the Lord *because He is holy.* Good worship begins with adoration, with praising God for who He is. Adoration serves as a springboard to cause worship to move up and away—up toward God and away from our preoccupation with ourselves.

Praising God for What He Has Done

Besides praising God for who He is, we also worship Him for what He does. God did not create us only to abandon us to fend for ourselves. He is busy caring for His people and His world. Adoration rightly acknowledges the blessings God sends our way. We praise Him for benefits such as forgiveness, healing, redemption, satisfaction, and renewal. For all of these and more He deserves praise. So we adore God because of His mighty deeds. "I will meditate on all your works and consider all your mighty deeds. . . . You are the God who performs miracles; you display your power among the peoples," writes the psalmist (Ps. 77:12, 14).

"We go to worship to praise and thank God for what he has done, is doing, and will do"[10]—as a result, we recognize His timelessness. We praise Him for the past, the present, and the future. Remembrance of what God has done, reflection upon how He presently blesses, and hopeful rejoicing in what He promises makes adoration an exercise by which we adopt an eternal perspective. The words of Heb. 12:28 reveal the attitude of expectancy in our praise: "Therefore, since we are receiving a kingdom that cannot be shaken, let us be thankful, and so worship God acceptably with reverence and awe."

False Starts in Worship

You've witnessed the Olympic games in which sprinters are called to the starting line. They carefully position themselves in the blocks, knowing the race is often won or lost in the start. They ready themselves, every muscle taut, as they listen for the starter's pistol. Often one or more will jump the gun and start before the others. A second chance is given. The whole process of positioning all runners starts again.

In leading worship, there are no chances for a restart. Yet, like the sprinter in the Olympics, a good or bad start in worship often determines whether we win or lose. When worship services have a false start—a focus other than God—the results are undesirable. We get sidetracked, if not totally derailed, from our purpose of glorifying Him. This is especially easy to do if we get lost in our own needs and concerns. Self-centered thinking, which replaces God-centered focus, is "the heart of our present crisis in worship."[11] Beginning a service of worship by focusing on ourselves, or anything else except God alone, severely subverts that grand purpose, the majestic vision, and the focus that worship must provide.

The Attitude of the Leaders of Worship

Since adoration and praise represent the proper foundation for worship, it is essential that this part of the service start with energy and positive excitement. Having led many worship services and worshiped in many others, I see repeatedly how the worship leader gets back from the congregation what he or she gives them by way of attitude and energy. Let me illustrate. If upon meeting John I flash him a big smile, I can almost be assured his response will be to return my greeting warmly. My action draws from John a positive response. If, on the other hand, I give John a scowl and a look of disdain, he will respond to me likewise. Congregations reflect what worship leaders give them—good attitudes or bad.

Because of this reflection response, we as worship leaders must be prepared to begin praise and adoration with positive energy and enthusiasm. We draw out enthusiastic response from worshipers by our demeanor. I like the word "enthusiasm." It is a compound word created from two words: *en*, which means "in" and *theos*, which is the Greek word for "God." So to be enthused is to have God in us. What better way to begin worship than to let God, who dwells within, show himself through our positive enthusiasm?

You know the schedule of many pastors. Sometimes we drag ourselves to the pulpit, exhausted before we begin. The "reflection response" means that the service is probably doomed to mediocrity. Our busyness can defeat us before we start.

If fatigue causes us to crawl through worship with no energy to give, we should stop and reprioritize. We adjust our Saturday evening schedule. We decide to decline weekend invitations. Whatever the particulars, we must find a way to be rested enough to lead worship with positive energy and enthusiasm. If we choose to make worship a priority, our example will train others well. (Who among us hasn't been frustrated by those attending Saturday night Sunday School class parties who are then too exhausted to find their way to Sunday morning worship?) God deserves the best we have to give. Enthusiastic and positive praise is a foundation upon which good worship is built.

Good worship causes us to reexamine ourselves and leads us to *confession and pardon.*

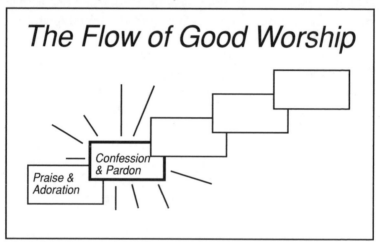

The Flow of Good Worship

Confession & Pardon

Praise & Adoration

Moving to Confession

Good worship focuses first on God's majestic holiness. It then challenges us to reexamine ourselves. When we catch a glimpse of the majestic holiness of God, we are confronted with our intense need for forgiveness and mercy. This thwarts our natural tendency to compare ourselves only with other persons. "Most people repent of their sins by thanking God they ain't [sic] so wicked as their neighbors," observes Josh Billings. If we keep our self-assessment on the human level, we can carefully choose to compare ourselves only with those who make us feel good about ourselves. But good worship naturally challenges us to measure ourselves by the Holy One. It moves from a vision of God's holiness to an awareness of our fallenness. Adoration and praise of our holy God lay the foundation for recognizing our sins, confessing them, and finding pardon.

In confession we lead our people to admit and turn away from our fallenness. As David Seamands reminds us, "We cannot confess to God what we do not acknowledge to ourselves."[12] Sensing and admitting that we come short of the glory of God is necessary before we can discover God's forgiving grace. Without the pain of confession, there can be no joy of grace.

Confession Is More than "I'm Sorry"

Someone suggested that the hardest words to utter are "I was wrong. Please forgive me." No doubt it's tough to admit our failures. But the English word "confession" means more than just "I was wrong." It has other related yet distinct shades of meaning in the Bible. The word translated "confess" is from the Hebrew *yada*. A primary meaning of this word, *yada*, is "to acknowledge or confess sin." But the word also means "to confess God's character and works."[13] This aspect of the word's meaning is easy to miss. To admit our sins to God is also to acknowledge His mercy and trustworthiness. He is one in whom we can depend. So confession includes more than acknowledging sin. Positively, confession means we realize we can find in God forgiving mercy.

Isaiah's Scriptural Model

The flow of worship is clearly seen in Isaiah's Temple vision. He models confession for us, showing how worshipers should respond to a holy God: "'Woe to me!' I cried. 'I am ruined! For I am a man of unclean lips, and I live among a people of unclean lips, and my eyes have seen the King, the LORD Almighty'" (Isa. 6:5). Witnessing the angelic beings worshiping God and seeing the majesty of God himself, Isaiah faces his own sinfulness.

In addition to his own fallenness, Isaiah clearly sees that the plight of all people is having fallen far short of God's holiness. Isaiah feels the heaviness of his own sin and, in a corporate sense, the fallenness of all humanity. His confession shows his desire for forgiveness and cleansing that leads to a restored relationship with God. Isaiah shows us that in confession we begin moving back to the holy God of love. By sorrowfully turning away from sin, we acknowledge the error in our lives, and we praise God by affirming His mercy. When we turn back to God in confession, the Holy One is praised as trustworthy, merciful, forgiving, and wanting to receive us back to himself. Confession acknowledges sin while praising the awesome character of God.

The Pastor as Priest

As the flow of worship causes the people to face their sin and need for repentance, the pastor assumes an important priestly role. The minister's pronouncement of God's forgiveness once confession occurs adds an essential aspect of Christian worship. By pronouncing forgiveness, the minister reminds the worshiper that God does indeed graciously extend His love.

But the worship leader-priest not only pronounces that truly penitent believers are indeed reconciled to God but also extends the challenge to live a holy and more Christlike life from this point forward. The natural place in the service for this to happen is in the pastoral prayer. A prayer like this might be voiced: *Father, for every person who genuinely turns from his or her sins to Christ Jesus this day, let that person experience the peace and joy of your forgiveness and grace. Give us victory over sin, and enable us to offer ourselves fully to righteousness, living holy lives that honor your name.* As Christ admonished the forgiven adulteress, we, too, can challenge the congregation to "Go, and sin no more." Only when this pattern has been completed is the worshiping community prepared to proceed with meaningful worship. Robert Webber comments,

> I now find that when I attend a church where I'm not led into preparation for worship, I am not ready to hear the Word of God. After all, I have come to that worship service with my burdens and needs. My life during the previous week has been rushed and hectic. I have done things that I should not have done, and I have left undone other things that I should have done. I need time to lay my burdens at the feet of Jesus. I need to be still and know that God is God. I need to hear him say, "You are forgiven. . . . You are my child. . . . I love you."[14]

Is There Any Sense of Sin?

Observations I've made when I am away from the church I pastor have helped my understanding of worship. I have visited various congregations across the nation in order to worship with them and to evaluate their services of worship. It has been fascinating to see the various ways other believers worship God. But many times I have come away from those services with a haunting sense that in North American Protestant churches we have lost any sense of the awfulness of sin. We typically assume the attitude "I'm OK—you're OK." Many services are conducted as if everyone present is good and there is simply no sin problem. Many of the services I have visited never mention sin at all!

John Wesley's prayers provide a stark contrast to this tendency to overlook sin. His call for sinners to wake up and realize our fallenness and our need to confess humbly our transgressions is a precursor to the discovery of God's marvelous forgiveness. How can there be any real sense of grace if there is no sense of the seriousness of sin? Consider the public prayer Wesley used to guide worshipers to confess their sin before the Holy One:

> Almighty and most merciful Father, we have erred and strayed from thy ways like lost sheep. We have followed

41

too much the devices and desires of our own hearts. We have offended against thy holy laws. We have left undone those things which we ought to have done; and we have done those things which we ought not to have done; and there is no health in us. But thou, Lord, have mercy upon us, miserable offenders. Spare thou them, God, which confess their faults. Restore thou them that are penitent; according to thy promises declared unto mankind in Christ Jesus our Lord. And grant, most merciful Father, for his sake, that we may hereafter live a godly, righteous, and sober life; to the glory of thy holy Name. Amen.[15]

This prayer acknowledges the sins of waywardness, improper desires, and disobedience. Admitting that things that should have been done have been omitted, there is acknowledgment of transgression of God's holy law. It includes "sins properly so called" and those "improperly so called"[16] (Wesley's terminology) and positions the worshipers in humble, sorrowful repentance before a holy God. Yet the attitude is not that of a rebel but of a child of God in need of forgiveness and restoration. The same attitude is illustrated in the prayer Jesus taught His disciples, "Forgive us our sins, for we also forgive everyone who sins against us" (Luke 11:4). As we confess our sin and turn from our waywardness, God forgives and restores.

Attitudes Toward Confession

There are many contrasting attitudes about the need for continued confession. One attitude I have seen grows from a strange and unhealthy twist that has occurred in the minds of some people. A longtime church member expressed the following sentiment when discussing the role of confession in the worship of the believer. She commented, "Since I am sanctified, I no longer sin. Therefore, I don't have anything I need to confess." (I have to admit I wanted to run to her husband and children to see if they saw her as flawless as she saw herself.) Please understand—the Bible clearly proclaims the possibility of both forgiveness and of freedom from continuing sin. Yet the attitude that we no longer need the cleansing of Christ's blood, that we have somehow progressed spiritually beyond the need for humble confession, is the height of prideful sin. It is far from responsible Holiness teaching.

The second attitude is quite different, and I have witnessed it in those longtime believers whose shining faces testify that they know God intimately. The peace, joy, and radiance that flows from them evidences their close walk with Jesus. You can likely put a name with the person I describe—you know folks like this too. It is that dear individual whose life evidences a breathing example of godliness. Rather than denying their need of confession, they possess an intense awareness of their coming up short. These saints not only refuse to deny their need but also seem much more intensely and painfully aware of it than many of the rest of us. As these Christians move closer to God, two things seem to happen: To those around them, these godly people seem to become more and more like the God they serve. But in their own eyes, as they move closer to God, they more clearly see just how much His holiness differentiates them from Him. A good way to describe their attitude is "humble holiness."

Recovering a Sense of Humility

A beautiful pattern in Paul's inspired writings that illustrates humble holiness is uncovered for us by William Barclay. "In the spiritual biography of Paul," he writes, "there is a strange progression." The progression shows how Paul saw himself spiritually. In Galatians, written around A.D. 48, Paul immediately lays claim to the highest title in the Church—"apostle." Writing to the Corinthians about seven years later, Paul then says, "I am the least of the apostles" (1 Cor. 15:9). Still eight years later (about A.D. 63), when writing to the Ephesian believers, he says of himself, "I am less than the least of all God's people" (Eph. 3:8). Finally, in a closing testimony Paul says to Timothy while awaiting death,

"Here is a trustworthy saying that deserves full acceptance: Christ Jesus came into the world to save sinners—of whom I am the worst" (1 Tim 1:15). What a fascinating progression—"apostle"—"least of the apostles"—"least of all God's people"—"worst of sinners" (v. 1:16).

The longer Paul lived for Christ, the less willing he was to claim for himself any spiritual commendation or position. Barclay observes, "The longer a man knows Jesus Christ, and the nearer he comes to Jesus Christ, . . . he is bound to see more and more clearly that standard of perfection in Christ by which he must judge his own life. A man may think he does a thing well—until some day he sees a real expert doing it; and then he knows how inadequate his own standard of performance is."[17]

A Pastoral Challenge: Teaching Confession Without Encouraging Sin

Those of us charged with leading God's people in worship have a tremendous obligation and opportunity to teach our people. Christians never outgrow the need to bow humbly before God and confess their need for forgiveness and continual cleansing. We must admit our falling short of God's magnificent glory. If we neglect this pastoral teaching obligation, we will develop not maturing saints, but pride-filled Pharisees. Yet when teaching people that we never outgrow the need of confession, we must do so in a manner that does not convey that intentional sin is the norm of Christian living. Since our God is a holy God, we are called to holy living.

Good worship leads us first to a vision of His holiness. Seeing our intense need for forgiveness and continual cleansing is a next natural step in the flow of worship. But with the awareness of our need for forgiveness and the confession through which God graciously pardons, good worship also confronts us with the call to live a holy life, to go and sin no longer. Through confession we find forgiveness and sense God's reconciling love. The grace, pardon, and restoration we find when we turn to God naturally leads to the next step in the flow of good worship.

Good worship inspires us to *thank God* for His great blessings.

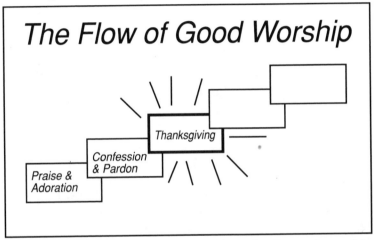

The Flow of Good Worship

Thanksgiving

Confession & Pardon

Praise & Adoration

Following confession and pardon, the flow of worship moves to thanksgiving. One friend who came to find Christ and the forgiveness of salvation described his experience as feeling "like a sack of cement has been lifted from my chest." The relief of sins forgiven is a miraculous blessing, and it is marvelous joy to discover that once we confess our need, God mercifully takes us to himself as His very own children. In continued confession that is repeated in worship, our place as God's child is reaffirmed. We sense again that we are a part of the family of God. This liberating experience of security naturally leads to joyous thanksgiving—God's people declaring from grateful hearts His goodness. Since thanksgiving focuses on God, it is closely related to adoration.

Many opportunities in worship enable worshipers to give thanks. In the pastoral prayer, gratitude to God for His gifts should be offered. Through hymns and choruses, the people can sing their thanks together. In public testimonies God's people have the opportunity to give Him thanks. The offering is itself an act of thanksgiving. God is gratefully praised for what He has provided, even as we trust Him to provide for the future. In thanksgiving God's people together declare "God is good." Because He is good, He deserves thanks. Because God is good, the people of the world deserve to know—to know what He has done and, more important, to know Him through Jesus Christ. The goodness of God, especially as He has revealed himself in Christ Jesus, must be shared. This flows into the next movement of good worship—proclamation.

Good worship includes a clear *proclamation of the gospel.*

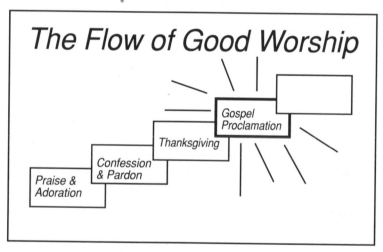

If the joy of God's forgiving grace leads us to give Him thanks, it should also cause us to tell others what a wonderful God we serve. In thanksgiving worshipers address God. In proclaiming the gospel we declare God's great love to those who need to know Him. To those who do not yet know Christ as Redeemer, proclamation attempts to make known what a wonderful, loving, and merciful God we serve. By retelling the greatest love story ever told, we let people know how much God loves them. In sending His Son to be born in Bethlehem, in Christ's living, dying, and being raised again, God shows us His love. Proclaiming the gospel faithfully lets the world know that "God the Father has come to us in His Son Jesus Christ to offer us newness of life, forgiveness, freedom and love."[18] The joyful experience of sins forgiven can be felt by all. Preaching the gospel, in which Jesus Christ is presented as the answer to our deepest needs, is a central part of good worship.

Proclamation of the gospel has long been central to Protestant worship. Since the Reformation, Protestant worship has emphasized the centrality of God's Word. Even the center placement of the pulpit emphasizes the importance of the Word. In some cases, the primacy of the Word in worship has been so great that services have been thought of in terms of "preliminaries" and sermon. Protestantism appears to be coming to a greater appreciation of the wider dimensions of worship. While an understanding of the flow of good worship elevates the preliminaries to a position of greater importance, it does not demote or diminish the value of the Word of God. Through proclamation of the Word, God speaks to His people. Proclamation actually serves two essential functions. In proclamation of the Word, nonbelievers are presented with the good news of Jesus Christ. *Evangelism* is a key function of proclamation. But proclamation also serves to build up or *edify* those who have already committed themselves to Christ Jesus. In the proclamation of the gospel, God still confronts us with our need for Him.

In our sanctuary hangs a large banner with these words: "Together . . . Winning the Lost, Building the Found." Our motto tries to keep our mission before the people. It emphasizes the same two functions proclamation strives to accomplish—evangelism (winning the lost) and edification (building the found). Both functions must occur if the Church is to accomplish its long-range mission.

While it is tempting to think of proclamation only in terms of the sermon, the Church can also proclaim God's deeds in other ways. Besides through preaching, proclamation takes place through the public reading of the Scriptures and by hymns and songs of the faith in which the message of the efforts of God on behalf of His people are sung. Drama is another means by which the gospel can be announced. In the sacraments of baptism and the Lord's Supper the redemptive deeds of God are proclaimed. In powerful symbolism the sacraments declare what God has done, is doing, and one day will do.

Just before we received the elements of Communion one Sunday morning, I offered this invitation: "If you have never invited Jesus Christ into your heart, you can do so right now. You could pray like this—'Lord, I realize I am a sinner and need your forgiveness. I turn from my sin. Forgive me and become my Lord.'"

"If you pray this prayer," the invitation continued, "join us in receiving the bread and the juice, letting this celebration of the Lord's Supper be for you the first outer sign of the commitment you have made with God today."

That night a young lady returned to our service. She had just started attending our services. During a time of testimonies, she quickly stood and quietly told us that Christ became her Lord just before she participated with us in Communion that morning. She prayed, and Christ transformed her life. This young woman went on to become an important part of that congregation, eventually serving on the church board. The same God who gave us the sacraments still works through them today to communicate His grace.

An example of biblical "proclamation" in which the mighty acts of God are recited is seen in Ps. 136. This psalm picks up the phrase "His love endures forever" and uses it as a refrain that responds to the praiseworthy deeds of God. Twenty-six times in the 26 verses the phrase "His love endures forever" is repeated. The psalm could well have first been written to lead worshipers in giving thanks for what God had done. It also reminds them that His love never fails.

As the psalm reminds the congregation of God's never-failing love, those outside the community of faith hear of the glorious goodness of God. When His goodness is proclaimed, wise hearers will want to know Him better. This leads us to the concluding move of good worship.

Good worship leads worshipers to deeper and fuller *commitment* **to God's will and purposes for us in Christ Jesus.**

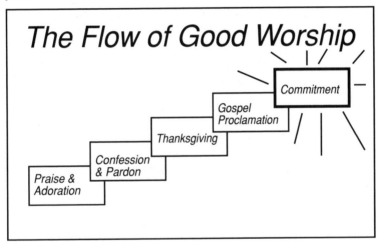

The Flow of Good Worship

Commitment

Gospel Proclamation

Thanksgiving

Confession & Pardon

Praise & Adoration

We know the importance of giving persons an opportunity to accept Christ as their Lord near the end of our services. Yet it seems odd that we often ignore the spiritual needs of those who have already accepted Christ as their Savior. Seeing commitment only in terms of an evangelistic response is like saying that if we have already turned to Christ, there is no more that God wants to do in our lives. Worshipers can be left with the impression of having no more obligation to God.

Evangelistic invitations are essential to the life of the Church. To forsake calling people to come to God in Christ

Jesus is to forsake our mission. On the other hand, if we take the New Testament as our model, we see that much of what is written there is not to the unbeliever but to those who have already accepted Christ. Those believers needed instruction and help to live out the gospel in their everyday lives. Similarly today, believers must be called to deeper and more complete commitment to God.

Good worship progressively flows so that participants, believers and unbelievers alike, move toward offering themselves to God. Beginning with adoration, moving through confession, thanksgiving, and proclamation of the gospel, the worship service naturally presses toward commitment. A well-known definition of worship by Archbishop William Temple expresses this movement: "To worship is to quicken the conscience by the holiness of God, to feed the mind with the truth of God, to purge the imagination by the beauty of God, to open the heart to the love of God, *to devote the will to the purpose of God.*"[19]

Temple's concept of worship rightly begins with the holiness of God. Worship then leads the congregation into those experiences that move toward a "devotion of the will to the purpose of God." Culminating in the moment in which devotion of the will occurs, commitment includes both self-surrender and adoption of the purposes of God in the world. Commitment ends the idolatry in which our selfish plans take priority. When we set these aside in order to take up God's aims and purposes, good worship—*real worship*—has happened. In commitment we devote ourselves to participate in Kingdom purposes and to share in the mission of Christ.

In effect, commitment means to pray as our Lord prayed—"Not my will, but yours be done" (Luke 22:42). Isaiah reports his call to commitment: "Then I heard the voice of the Lord saying, 'Whom shall I send? And who will go for us?' And I said, 'Here am I. Send me!'" (Isa. 6:8). But the call to commitment was not to Isaiah alone. It was for all of us

who genuinely worship. "Every significant worship experience calls for submission and surrender to the will of God.
The encounter in worship is incomplete if it does not lead to
surrender."[20] If worship is truly effective, it will lead participants to deeper commitment.

Robert Webber discusses commitment in terms of
"covenant." An essential aspect of worship in both the Jew-
ish and Christian traditions is the continuous renewal of personal commitment. In worship the community engages in renewing the covenant that exists between God and itself.[21]

Commitment to God in worship is a lifelong process.
Certainly there is that initial moment in which we first surrender our will to God and become disciples of Christ. But
commitment is more than a one-time act. Our commitment is
repeatedly renewed in worship. In commitment, we reaffirm
our surrender and our determination to hear, serve, and obey.
If there is no commitment in the worship experience, serious
problems arise. Without the challenge of commitment, the
worship service degenerates into an exercise in religious entertainment. Without commitment, worshipers become spectators—religious consumers—who feel free to judge the performance of the up-front people, much as television critics
evaluate the new season's shows. Along with an attitude of
noncommitment comes a tendency to go where the best religious show is occurring. Rather than faithfulness to a specific
congregation, the lack of commitment becomes religious consumerism that denies and destroys any chance of real fellowship. Many claim that religious consumerism strongly influences evangelical worship in the United States today. Such an
approach to discipleship makes true worship impossible.
Apart from commitment, worship's power to transform lives
by renewing awareness of God's glory fades.

Religious consumers will never know the joy that
comes to those who worship God in spirit and truth. Without
commitment to the One who alone deserves reverence, glory,
and praise, lasting peace is bartered for a momentary senti-

mental feeling. By contrast, true worship challenges and leads those present to continuing commitment and self-surrender.

Conclusion

What is to happen when we worship? The simple answer is that God is to be glorified. Both Scripture and the history of worship show us more. Some clear and positive elements of good worship make it possible for a flow to occur in a well-led service. From adoration and praise of our holy God, we come face-to-face with ourselves as we are. Our confession of our sinfulness is met with divine pardon and cleansing. Thanksgiving results; and in our joy, we want and need to tell others in gospel proclamation how wonderful God is. When the great and good God we serve is proclaimed, others will want to commit their lives to Him, and believers will want to draw even nearer.

The patterns shaping good worship should be kept clearly in mind by those who lead our services. By understanding these patterns, we have greater freedom to shape worship responsibly. By understanding what lies behind good worship, those who worship—and those of us charged with the responsibility of leading worship—are set free to honor the Lord in ways that both glorify Him and build up those who praise His name. By keeping the shaping patterns of good worship in mind, we can avoid dangerous fads and see that God is allowed His rightful place—first place—in our services and our lives. As C. S. Lewis said, "The perfect church service would be one we were almost unaware of: our attention would have been on God."[22]

3

Seekers or Saved? Where's the Human Focus of Worship?

WHILE GOD MUST REMAIN THE CENTER OF TRUE worship, the human side of worship planning can't be ignored. Even God-centered worship takes place with people—people God loves. He has acted to save all who come to Him. Without people, there is no corporate worship. When we begin to consider the human side of worship planning, we quickly realize we face a choice: Will our services target seekers, or will they be designed for those who are already saved?

A Contemporary Problem with Age-old Roots

If you have wrestled with the problem of who to target in your services, take heart—you're not alone. Many others facing the weekly planning of worship services struggle with this issue. "In each Sunday morning congregation sit many for whom Jesus is not yet Lord. Whatever their reasons for attending, they have come more to observe than to worship. Their presence presents worship leaders with a challenge: How can we involve non-Christians in a service in which the main act is the worship of

Christ?"[1] Robert Webber struggles with the same question, asking how believers' worship is related to evangelism.[2]

Identifying the target audience of our services is complicated by the mission of the Church, which includes evangelizing the lost. To worship without concern for evangelism is sub-Christian. To focus only on evangelism without offering believers opportunity to worship God is likewise unacceptable. God calls His Church to do both.

This dilemma has ancient roots. In the Early Church the problem was handled by making a clear distinction between full members, who were fully committed to Christ, and seekers or novices in the faith, who were identified as probationary members. The seekers and recently converted were allowed to participate only in the early portions of the worship. Near the end of the services when only full members celebrated the Lord's Supper, seekers and newly converted probationary members were escorted out to receive instruction in the Scripture, Christian living, and prayer. After three years of training, new converts were baptized and admitted to the full membership of the church. Only then could they participate in the believers' worship.[3]

We've already discussed John Wesley's dilemma of taking the gospel to the unchurched masses in 18th-century England. When he developed the strategy of field preaching, he was not envisioning a new form of worship but an effective method of evangelizing. Wesley realized the importance of the Church's doing more than simply maintaining itself through worship by believers. The history of Protestant Christianity shows many cases in which church leaders have chosen to focus services on either evangelism or worship. Apparently many generations of Christians have struggled to find the right balance between believer-sensitive worship and seeker-sensitive evangelism.

Our Continuing Challenge

A major challenge for church leaders is to design appropriate worship services that effectively lead already-committed Christians to glorify God and grow in their faith without ignoring those who still need to accept Jesus Christ. Services that focus only on the already-converted cut short the church's evangelistic mission of winning the lost. On the other hand, services that focus only on winning the lost may leave the already-converted feeling they have completed their obligation to God when they accept Christ as their Savior.

Our Commitment to the Already-Converted

Our commitment to those who have committed their lives to Jesus Christ says that we should not expect them to conform their worship totally to the tastes and expectations of the unbelieving visitor. If worship is made servant to the preferences of those who have made no commitment to God, we cut ourselves loose from our foundations and all that is lasting, dependable, and secure. No sooner do we complete a design of worship services based on current preferences than we find preferences shift and our faddish style passé.

The issue is really deeper than current preferences. Much of what is, or is not, acceptable in worship must be evaluated according to the guidelines of God's holy Word. When we cut ourselves loose from clear guidance found in God's Word and elevate current cultural preferences to the place of control, we set ourselves up for catastrophe. Yet when we blindly ignore the needs and preferences of contemporary society, we isolate ourselves from a viable future.

Our Commitment to the Not-Yet-Saved

To commit ourselves solely to shape worship according to the preferences of those who have already given themselves to Jesus Christ is to ignore the needs of the not-yet-saved. It is easy for the already-converted to find ample evidence in their examination of Scripture to endorse their own traditional patterns and practices of worship. Yet the Lord who told us that "the Son of Man came to seek and to save what was lost" (Luke 19:10) wants us to concern ourselves with evangelizing those who have yet to turn to Him. Tradition is powerful and can sometimes prohibit God from touching lives as He desires.

Our Goal

Since worship *and* evangelism are essential to the life of Christ's Body, the goal is to provide services that target two groups: We must provide services that effectively lead believers to glorify God. These services are oriented toward the already-committed and provide the opportunity for edification and growth. Other services must give seekers a genuine opportunity to understand the gospel and accept Christ as Lord. Evangelism is the key to these services. Seeker-sensitivity becomes essentially important.

Many believe that both worship and evangelism cannot be effectively done in one service. Rick Warren, pastor of Saddleback Community Church in Orange County, California, suggests that if most churches instituted in their traditional service what it takes to reach unbelievers, many worshipers would revolt![4] (In making this point, Warren also raises the hot issue of styles of worship in which tradition often finds itself at odds with the needs of the surrounding culture. We'll discuss this later.) Bill Hybels, pastor of Willow Creek Community Church, says, "You cannot do evangelism and edification optimally at the same time, in the same place, in the same meeting."[5] Commenting on Hybels's statement, George Hunter says of the church Hybels leads, "[Willow Creek Community Church] discovered that . . . if you focus a service for believers, the visiting seekers feel left out and that Christianity doesn't apply to them. If you focus on the seekers, the believers who need the meat of Scripture will feel like they are malnourished inside. If you shoot for the middle, you miss both populations.[6]

Willow Creek's solution to this problem is to use weekends (they have both Saturday and Sunday services) as the time for evangelizing. Their seeker-sensitive services intentionally target the unconverted. Wednesday and Thursday night services, called New Community Services, serve to edify and nurture those who already believe in Christ.

This is not to say that a worship service cannot have evangelistic impact. When God's people come together with hearts and minds eager and ready to glorify the Lord, their authentic worship can still communicate God and His love to contemporary culture. Yet Christians through the ages have recognized that worship services are distinct in purpose from services focusing on evangelism.

A Possible Solution

Many churches are already in a favorable position to respond to this dilemma because they hold services on both Sunday morning and evening. It would be a very natural move for many congregations to focus on evangelism of nonbelievers on Sunday morning while designating the Sunday evening as the worship service targeting believers.

Why evangelize on Sunday morning? There are good reasons—at least in our local church. My personal observation is that many choose to attend only one service each week. If people choose only one service to attend, frequently it is Sunday morning. The primary reason to reach out to the lost on Sunday morning is because that is when those who are uncommitted are more likely to be present. Newcomers, as well as fringe persons from the congregation, who need Christ attend more on Sunday morning than at any other time. A fisherman knows you'll catch more if you dangle your bait where the fish are present. If we are going to win persons to Christ in our services, we had better do it when they are present!

Some congregations have already adopted a twofold approach to their services similar to what is proposed. Robert Webber observes that more and more churches are distinguishing between a seekers' service and believers'

worship. The first is aimed at bringing unbelievers into relationship with Christ, while the latter purpose seeks to
help those who have already committed to Christ to grow.[7]
The proposed schedule can be diagrammed like this:

Schedule	*Purpose*	*Target Audience*
Sunday morning	Evangelism	Seekers
Sunday evening	Worship and Edification	Believers

Suggestions for Planning

Five specific suggestions can be made to improve
worship planning:

● **Know your focus group and your purpose.** If the
focus group is the *not-yet-converted,* plan services that are
seeker-sensitive. Our aim is to win a hearing of the
gospel—to let its power work in the lives of those to whom
God will speak.

If the focus of the service is *believers,* plan to lead them
to worship and praise that moves to a deeper commitment
to God in Christ Jesus. Our aim is to glorify the King of
Kings. Worship is not an end in itself. By exalting Him, we
are challenged and changed to live more fully committed
to His purposes and will.

Without losing focus, *be flexible.* It's OK to offer opportunities for coming to Christ even in services of worship.
When God's people come together to exalt God genuinely,
to celebrate what He has done, is doing, and will do, God
can powerfully communicate through our worship to
those who have yet to commit themselves to Christ. While
this may not be the primary time when we evangelize or
when most seekers are present, there may be occasions
when the Holy Spirit opens doors of invitation we dare not
close. On these occasions, sensitivity to God's leading can
tell us when to "draw the net." We must not be so rigid

that we refuse to allow God freedom to expand the focus of our services. On the other hand, to have a fuzzy focus or no focus is to abdicate our responsibility to carry forth two of the essential elements of the Church's mission: worship and evangelism.

● **Emphasize worship by establishing specific services for believers to gather and praise God.** If we really believe in the importance of worship, then the pastor must assume responsibility for leading the church in worship.

Worship is not natural. We must learn how to glorify the Lord. As worship leaders, we are responsible to teach what worship is and how to do it. When we come together with a clearly understood and singular purpose, we can more easily guide our people into good patterns of worship.

● **Provide designated seeker-sensitive services and train believers to bring their unsaved friends to these services.** I have been amazed at how willingly people respond when trusted leadership offers a clear vision of where we are headed and "handles" that make uniting behind the vision possible. Many times our people don't do what we desire simply because we have not told them what we want. In designating a particular weekly service as seeker-sensitive, I'm suggesting that there be a designated service time when we tell our folks, "This is the best time to bring your friends." In designating a seeker-sensitive service, I'm suggesting that we try to be aware of how new people not familiar with our worship patterns and procedures may feel when they enter our church services. The degree to which the emphasis is placed on seeker-sensitivity is a matter for each pastor and congregation to decide. It is also a matter of understanding the surrounding culture to better know what the people to whom your church seeks to reach are like.

One example of an attempt to be seeker-sensitive is the approach to welcoming visitors. While differing patterns seem to work in various places, we have found a procedure that works well for us in balancing the tension between offering a warm, friendly welcome and allowing visitors to feel not so conspicuous. Before visitors enter the sanctuary, a parking lot greeter welcomes them. They are guided to the foyer of the sanctuary, where they meet other greeters who get their names and addresses. A small sunflower, a symbol of our state, is placed onto their clothing to identify them as visitors. In our service we welcome our visitors and invite them to stay for a meal we call "Lunch Bunch." Then I say something like this: "Would all those who consider this your regular church home please stand? Those seated around you are your guests. Greet them warmly, and let them know how pleased you are they've come." We then allow a few moments when our congregation reaches out to those who visit. Because the visitors have been allowed to remain seated, they feel less conspicuous and yet are greeted warmly.

This is not a radical interpretation of seeker-sensitivity. Some suggest far more. For some, seeker-sensitivity means heavy use of drama. For others, seeker-sensitivity means replacing traditional hymns and gospel songs with more contemporary music. For some, it means opting for a low-key approach to finances. Seeker-sensitivity can mean many things to many people.

Likewise, approaches to evangelism vary. To designate a service as "seeker-sensitive" and to call it a time of evangelism can conjure up competing images. For some, a direct, frontal assault in which nonbelievers are confronted with their waywardness and are called to immediate repentance may be the preferred and most effective method. Others find that the people they are trying to reach, and who have no religious memories on which to draw, need time to reflect and think through the implications of the new gospel message they hear. It may take months of listening, watching, and thinking before they are ready to respond, and so a low-key, nonconfrontational approach is used. The unique mix of the pastor's personality and gifts, the congregation's traditional strengths, and the composition of the community means that no one approach is always right. Seeking God for the unique situation in which you minister is essential.

It should be obvious that all of these seeker-sensitive components taken together are radically different from what is traditionally experienced in many of our churches. Lyle Schaller offers some sage advice in his volume *Strategies for Change*. He suggests that effecting long-range change in the local church will have greater likelihood for success if the trusted pastor-leader takes a slower, incremental approach to instituting change as opposed to a revolutionary overthrow of the cherished patterns of the congregation.[8]

- **Aim for participation and interaction.** Most of us do similar things in our worship services. We sing, pray, give, and preach during our services. But while we do similar things, it is important that we remember those leading the services are not actors entertaining spectators, but rather, we are prompters seeking to lead our people to worship God themselves. Music is a key area in which this distinction makes a great difference. Is the purpose of the church's music to sing to the congregation through choirs and other special music? Or is a better approach to use the music to cause the congregation to get caught up in praise and adoration themselves? Good leadership in worship aims to involve the congregation in being worshipers and not spectators.

- **Seek to touch the emotions, mind, and will.** Simply put, if we can make them laugh, if we can make them cry, and if we can make them think, we will improve our chances of causing them to act on what they already feel and know. Some persons respond from a rational, logically oriented mind. Probably a larger group responds more naturally from their feelings. Most persons are a blend of both. If our services are to touch the most persons possible, it is important that we plan to let them feel and think as we challenge them clearly to commit their will to the Lordship of Christ.

Conclusion

Worship planning is a challenge for all worship leaders. We must continually examine our practices to seek to do the best we can to provide services that lead our people to glorify God while we remain sensitive to the needs of the not-yet-converted. Seekers or saved?—who is worship for? The answer lies in the God who reaches out in Christ Jesus to everyone and allows us to forget no one. Worship is for everyone!

4

What People Say About Worship

RIDING TO KINDERGARTEN ONE FOGGY MORNING, a little girl curiously asked, "Daddy, what is fog?"

Her father replied, "Meteorologically, we can say that fog occurs when a cloud of condensed water vapor in the form of water droplets or ice crystals is suspended in the atmosphere just over the surface of the earth."

A long pause followed. The little girl finally spoke: "Are you talking to me?"

No doubt, worship leaders are responsible to keep worship *God-centered*. But, even so, if worship is to connect, it must also be *person-oriented*. When people are forgotten in worship planning, the effect is like the dad who forgot he was answering his five-year-old daughter. Worship leaders are responsible to present worship in terms the people can understand and appreciate. Without God as its focus, worship is misdirected. Without a person-orientation, it becomes irrelevant.

If we are to develop and maintain an orientation toward people, we need to know their concerns in worship. I like the title of a current book: *How Will They Hear If We Don't Listen?* The desire to discover the thoughts of worshipers and potential worshipers led to the creation, distribution, and analysis of a survey on worship I conducted in 1992 in Wichita, Kansas. The goal was to gain perspective on the "view from the pew" relating to what is really important in worship. The survey respondents were nearly equally divided between those who were presently attending church and those who were not. What they told us has exciting and challenging implications for worship.

The purpose of collecting and examining this information was not to establish popular opinion as the determining factor in shaping corporate worship. Rather, the aim of the survey was to become more aware of what worshipers and potential worshipers say will enable them to experience greater fulfillment in services of worship. The compiled responses reveal some possible ways Christian corporate worship may better address the needs of persons. It also helps us see what some persons want to happen when they attend worship services.

Five Key Insights into Worship from a Worshiper's Perspective

The survey was devised in part to discover why respondents attend worship services. To ask why they come helps identify what they want and need from the services. The survey asked these persons to identify and rank from a list of 13 items the 5 most important to them as components of a typical church service. The responses were tabulated and given a weighted ranking. Each number-one ranking was given a value of three points, each number-two ranking a value of two points, and each number-three ranking one point. Responses of number-four and number-five rankings were not awarded value points in the weighted ranking.

The following data table shows the results of the compiled totals. They are placed in descending order, with the most important items toward the top.

Table 6: Respondents' Perceptions of Matters of Importance in a Church Service

Rank	Item	Weighted Rank
1	I want to worship God because He is God.	99
2	I want to offer thanks to God.	52
3	I want to hear what the Bible says.	42
4	I want to be challenged to live a more godly life.	37
5	I want to feel the love and support of the "church family."	30
6	I want to pray or learn to pray.	29
7	I want to find forgiveness for my sins.	27
8	I want to commit or recommit myself to God.	23
9	I want to hear a good sermon.	22
10	I want to prepare for life after death.	19
11	I want to learn to live more effectively.	15
12	I want an opportunity to become actively involved.	10
13	I want to be with my friends.	8

The following graph presents the relative strength of the respondents' top five reasons for attending church services.

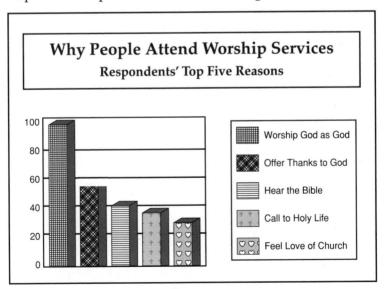

Why People Attend Worship Services
Respondents' Top Five Reasons

- Worship God as God
- Offer Thanks to God
- Hear the Bible
- Call to Holy Life
- Feel Love of Church

By analysis of the compiled responses, five statements of what these folks seek in worship emerge. For the pastors-worship leaders who want to keep in touch with their people, it seems wise to listen. Here are five key concerns expressed by worshipers and suggestions for addressing them.

"Keep the services centered on God." Seems too simple and obvious, doesn't it? Isn't God automatically the focus of worship?

It was Saturday evening in early July, and our family was vacationing in the southwestern United States. Cities were few—towns far apart. We knew we would worship tomorrow, but where? As one who preaches nearly every Sunday, I am eager to hear a good sermon on those occasions when I step away from my pulpit responsibilities. We carefully examined the map to locate the next town, where we would find a church in which to worship. Rising early, we arrived in town, found a beautiful, newly constructed, modern church building. It appeared to be just the place we had hoped to worship on this Lord's day morning. We eagerly entered the sanctuary and found our seats with a sense of anticipation.

The service started with a patriotic bent—not too surprising on this Sunday, the Fourth of July. Patriotic songs were followed by former servicemen who recounted stories of their wartime military experiences. Some were dressed in their uniforms. Poems were read praising and exalting our nation.

I waited for the service to turn to God. To my great disappointment, it never did. No reading from Scripture—no prayer time—no sermon. Jesus Christ was never mentioned. The Sunday morning service from start to finish was a celebration of nationalism. It ended with an invitation to attend the Independence Day hamburger cookout.

I believe our nation is a wonderful place in which to live. Our servicemen deserve honor and respect. Many sacrificed greatly to make us free. Without the commitment of those who serve in the armed forces, we would not enjoy the freedoms we have today. I, too, once proudly served my country in the military. History has shown that the freedoms we enjoy cost a great deal—for some, their very lives. I understand and believe this.

But in that service *where was God?* The focus of worship cannot be merely human experience, but rather must remain on Jesus Christ—His life, death, and resurrection. This service omitted God completely. God and His Son were left on the shelf until needed again. To remove God from the center of any service of worship is idolatrous. Without God there *is* no worship.

A poem found by the entrance to a village church says it well:

> *No man entering a house ignores him who dwells there.*
>
> *This is the house of God and he is here.*
>
> *Pray then to him who loves you and bids you welcome.*
>
> *Give thanks for those who in years past*
> *built this place to his glory.*
>
> *Rejoice in his gifts of beauty in art and music,*
> *architecture and handicrafts*
>
> *And worship him the one God and Father of us all*
>
> *through our Lord and Savior Jesus Christ. Amen.*[1]

Those who worship with us each week want God-centered worship services—they know the only right focus of worship is God in Christ Jesus. The first task of the worship leader is to unite the people's minds and hearts on Him. Worshipers arrive at church escaping distracting weeks in which they have been bombarded with frustrations. Even getting to the church is often stress-filled. Ask any mom with small children! Worship services that begin with the One who has all life in His control offer a refreshing and right perspective on our hectic days. He alone offers peace, life, wholeness, and strength. God alone must be at the center of our worship.

A second key reason people attend worship is because they want to express their gratitude. They say, **"Give us opportunity to express thanks to God."**

Remember the story of the 10 who were healed by Jesus? Of the 10 who were made well, only 1 returned to say "thanks." Preachers have often raised the issue of "Where were the other 9?" The question implies that the 9 (and maybe most of us) don't want to be thankful. The people who responded to the survey present a different possibility. Those responding to the question "Why do you attend services of worship?" said they wanted opportunity to give thanks to God. Maybe instead of a lack of desire to thank God for His blessings, people want help to do what they know they should. Perhaps they look to the time of worship for direction and the chance to be grateful.

Gratitude is a very difficult emotion for some to express. Sometimes we struggle to express what we feel deeply. Those whose lives have been transformed by Jesus Christ may experience this dilemma as they assemble to worship. The question then becomes, "How can we help worshipers express their feelings of gratitude?"

To respond to this question, it seems good to review scriptural passages that focus on thanksgiving. Apparently some worship activities are better suited to allowing God's people to express gratitude. Two scriptural insights are appropriate: First, especially in the Old Testament, *thankfulness is frequently associated with music.*

It is fascinating how often a thankful attitude is linked to music in worship. About one-fourth of the verses in the Old Testament that contain some form of the word "thanks" also include a reference to music. Sometimes it's a song of praise, sometimes a choir, and sometimes the playing of musical instruments that lifts grateful praise to God. Over and over, however, the clear connection between grateful people and music is obvious. Thankful people naturally express their gratitude through musical praise. Here are four Old Testament examples:

> The trumpeters and singers joined in unison, as with one voice, to give praise and thanks to the LORD. Accompanied by trumpets, cymbals and other instruments, they raised their voices in praise to the LORD and sang: "He is good; his love endures forever." Then the temple of the LORD was filled with a cloud. —2 Chron. 5:13

> After consulting the people, Jehoshaphat appointed men to sing to the LORD and to praise him for the splendor of his holiness as they went out at the head of the army, saying: "Give thanks to the LORD, for his love endures forever." —2 Chron. 20:21

> The LORD is my strength and my shield; my heart trusts in him, and I am helped. My heart leaps for joy and I will give thanks to him in song. —Ps. 28:7

> Sing to the LORD with thanksgiving; make music to our God on the harp. —Ps. 147:7

Apparently thankful people are singing people! With the Old Testament offering such strong indication that music is a primary medium of expressing thanks, it is wise for us to see music as a way to allow our people to express their gratitude to God today.

Scripture provides a second insight in leading our people in thanksgiving; in the New Testament (where thanksgiving's connection with music is less apparent), a thankful attitude is often expressed through prayer.

Looking at New Testament verses, these words challenge us:

> Be joyful always; pray continually; give thanks in all circumstances, for this is God's will for you in Christ Jesus. —1 Thess. 5:16-18

Devote yourselves to prayer, being watchful and thankful.
—Col. 4:2

Do not be anxious about anything, but in everything, by prayer and petition, with thanksgiving, present your requests to God.
—Phil. 4:6

Notice the pattern? Pray—*give thanks;* pray—*be thankful;* pray—*with thanksgiving.* Thanksgiving is expressed in prayer. In true prayer we express our gratitude for what God has already done and our trust that He will continue to bless us in the days to come. Chuck Swindoll says it well: "Thanksgiving is a much more important holiday than is the Fourth of July. On the Fourth of July, we celebrate our independence; but on Thanksgiving, we celebrate our dependence."[2]

Even the act of inviting our people to give thanks in prayer is an opportunity to focus on what is really important. We can lead our people to small-mindedness, to think on trivial things while ignoring essential issues. We can allow the tendency to focus on the physical, temporal, or material world to dominate even our thanksgiving. This problem of preoccupation with the physical world and things of lesser importance has crept into our prayer times. One longtime Christian writes,

> Within the span of my memory of the church, I believe I can detect a difference in soul burden as evidenced by the testimonies of the saints. Youthful recollection takes me back to days when the pastor asked the congregation for prayer requests, and one or more would rise, often in great emotional distress, to request prayer for an unsaved loved one or friend. Now that same opportunity is met with a request for someone who is physically ill.[3]

It is not that God does not care about our physical needs—He does. But it is possible that we allow issues of lesser importance to squeeze the most important issues out of our prayers and thanksgiving. When the temporary physical body is elevated to prominence over the eternal souls of persons, we have lost sight of what is ultimately important.

Congregations can be led to think in large-minded terms by following the lead of the Scripture. In Scripture, blessings such as God's grace, His covenant faithfulness, and the deliverance He gives in Christ Jesus are gratefully acknowledged. When examining the recorded prayers of Jesus, the great contrast with many of our prayers today becomes obvious. In the prayers of our Lord, instead of a concentrated focus on the physical side of life, we see essential, eternal, life-changing issues are His prime concern—issues like the holiness of God and the soon coming of His kingdom. We hear Jesus teaching us to pray for forgiveness and deliverance from temptation. He prays for the sanctification of His disciples and their effectiveness in carrying out the mission they have been given. He prays for our joy and for our protection from the evil one. He is concerned that we remain united and the world know that He has come with salvation. We hear Jesus praying that God's will be done, in spite of personal pain and inconvenience. These are neither small-minded nor trivial concerns. In guiding our people to thanksgiving for the most essential issues, we train them to think "with the mind of Christ," to think in terms of what really matters.

Songs and prayer are two primary means in Scripture by which God's people express their thanks to Him. If we are to make it easier for worshipers to thank God for the many blessings He gives, singing and praying are two main worship activities that can help us accomplish this goal.

"Let us hear God's Word." The service began with joyous praise and progressed smoothly toward the opening of God's Word to the congregants. Intuitively, we knew the reading of the Word and the sermon were coming. But this service would not include a mindless, unprepared reading of Scripture. The focus was the Book of Revelation. An individual dressed as the apostle John appeared, dramatically presenting the passage from which the pastor would momentarily speak. "The Revelator" spoke the Word with passion and deep feeling as if he were still exiled to the isle of Patmos. The power of the written Word roared to life for me as I not only heard the inspired words but saw them too. I suspect no one slept through that reading of Scripture![4]

Creativity usually shakes us loose from our "We've always done it that way" mentality. But while creative approaches to presenting God's Word get attention, for most congregations, most of the time, the people hear the Word of God through a more traditional public reading of Scripture and through the preaching of God's Word. How can we more effectively present God's Word in public worship? Let's consider these two related aspects of public worship.

Reading Scripture in Public

In a visually oriented society, it's easy to minimize the importance of publicly reading God's Word. Since reading Scripture is not filled with fast-changing visual images, some would discount its importance for today. Yet our people need to be exposed to the truths of God revealed in the public reading of Scripture. One nationwide survey reveals that of those who identified themselves as Christian, 42 percent said that in a typical week they *never read the Bible once outside of church*. Only 12 percent said they read it every day.[5] Even many church attenders hear God's Word only if presented in public worship. What can we do to elevate the importance of the Word in the minds of our people? Let's consider three simple suggestions:

1. *Train those who lead the public reading to preread the selected passage so they can read with confidence and clarity.* Since the written Word is worthy of respect and honor, the public reading of it should not be done haphazardly. The congregation will sense the Word is worthy of respect if it is read well. They will also perceive the unpreparedness of the leader if words are unfamiliar and names are bungled. Preparedness points to the importance of the public reading of Scripture.

2. *Have the congregation stand for the reading of the Word.* A worship custom worth cultivating is having worshipers stand when the Bible is read. In the Scripture describing the worship renewal that took place in the days of Nehemiah we find these words:

> Ezra opened the book. All the people could see him because he was standing above them; and as he opened it, the people all stood up. Ezra praised the LORD, the great God; and all the people lifted their hands and responded, "Amen! Amen!" Then they bowed down and worshiped the LORD with their faces to the ground. . . . They read from the Book of the Law of God, making it clear and giving the meaning so that the people could understand what was being read *(Neh. 8:5-6, 8)*.

I like Robert Webber's comment on this passage: "It is interesting to note all that is going on in this incident: the reader standing in a place where he could be seen; the people standing as the book was opened, lifting their hands, saying 'Amen,' bowing to the ground; the Levites reading, making it clear, giving the meaning; the people understanding." The people were active and involved as the Word of God was read. Webber concludes, "This was no passive mumbling of Scripture, no mere preliminary to the sermon!"[6]

The Early Christian Church likewise adopted the pattern of inviting worshipers to stand for the reading of the written Word. The point, however, is not what those who came before us have done. Rather, the issue is what can we do to enhance the importance of the Word in the minds of contemporary worshipers. Yet even today, standing for the public reading of the Scriptures signals that God's Word deserves honor and respect.

3. *Introduce the reading of Scripture with a statement signifying the honor it deserves.* After announcing the passage to be read, the importance of the reading of the Word can be emphasized with a simple statement signifying its importance. "This is God's Word" or "Hear the Word of the

Lord" are two examples. Both statements signal the importance of the Word by pointing to God as its source.

These three suggestions—mental, physical, and verbal—guide worshipers to sense the respect and honor the holy Word deserves. Through careful preparation, having the congregation stand, and prefacing the reading of the Word with a statement of its holy origin, we point worshipers toward increasing respect for the written Word.

Preaching God's Word

Wouldn't it be fascinating (or maybe frightening) to know how the sermons we preach are perceived by those who listen? Research reported by Wes Tracy in "What They Are Saying About Our Preaching"[7] gives us feedback from our hearers. Both pastors and laypersons were asked to share their perspectives on current pulpit fare. Six hundred randomly selected pastors and church members were surveyed, asking for their responses on 30 aspects of preaching. Preachers should be encouraged by what the people said about the preaching they hear. The overall tone of the responses was encouraging. But while the reports were largely positive, there are some concerns preachers should hear and heed. In the survey, laypersons were given opportunity to respond to the open-ended statement "If I could change one thing about most of the preaching I hear, it would be . . ." Tracy reports, "Exactly 111 lay respondents took time to write out 130 changes they would eagerly vote for. The runaway winner in the 'change one thing' contest was SHORTER SERMONS."[8] (I must admit sermons seem much longer when I listen to them than when I preach them. And my guess is that it has nothing to do with how well I preach!)

From the preacher's point of view, one item surfaced that deserves attention. The second-most desired change on the part of pastors was "more time for sermon preparation." Wes Tracy comments, "There was not a syllable, not the slightest hint in any layperson response that showed any awareness of this vital need of pastors."[9] Perhaps if we who preach intentionally set aside more time to prepare, we will be able to say more in less time and thus satisfy those who listen to us as well as meeting our own felt need!

The following table shows the top 10 responses of what church members most want to change about preaching, as reported in the study:

What Church Members Most Want to Change About Preaching

1. Shorter sermons
2. Better application to practical problems
3. More biblically based
4. More holiness doctrine
5. Evangelistic appeal
6. Simplicity
7. Fewer stories and illustrations
8. More spontaneous, less formal
9. Hear more of God's love
10. More expository preaching[10]

Preachers cannot let popular opinion control what and how we preach. Paul warned Timothy of this problem when he predicted that "the time will come when men will not put up with sound doctrine. Instead, to suit their own desires, they will gather around them a great number of teachers to say what their itching ears want to hear" (2 Tim. 4:3). Yet it is foolish to ignore the legitimate concerns of those who listen to sermons each week. By becoming more aware of what hearers perceive, we may better help them draw near to God.

Contemporary life demands more and more from workers—pastors included. Demands for administrative prowess, counseling skill, and a host of other things call for the pastor's time. Yet, for many, the call of God on our lives is a *call to preach.*

A seven-year-old child rode alone in the backseat of the brown '59 Oldsmobile. Scenery flew by the windows as Dad and Mom talked up front about the important things adults discuss. But the conversation in the backseat was more important. God was talking to the young boy. Inwardly the boy heard God's call to preach the good news of Jesus Christ. The boy leaned forward to announce to surprised parents (who weren't even churchgoers at the time), "When I grow up, I'm going to be a preacher."

I know that story, because it is mine. God's call on my life was a call to preach. He said nothing about administration, counseling, or guiding a local Christian education program—although the pastoral ministry demands all these roles. He did specifically call me to preach, however.

This experience influences my conviction that *nothing a pastor outwardly does is more important than the preaching of God's Word.* If the pastoral role we fill includes responsibilities in the pulpit, we must give priority to the preaching task. Thomas Oden reminds us that "preaching is the most public of pastoral acts. The quality and depth of Christian discipleship in a congregation depend heavily upon it."[11]

David Buttrick likewise challenges us to our calling:

> Luther said, "The church comes into being because God's Word is spoken." Nowadays, we do not understand Luther's astonishing confidence in the Word. As far as we can see, churches form and survive by management—attention to detail, successful promotion, and fiscal responsibility. . . . When tensions arise, a course in conflict management will come in handy; a wise preacher, we suppose, will never address issues publicly. So we have no vision of the Word at work sustaining and reforming the life of the church. Are we born too late to grasp Luther's sweeping confidence?[12]

What is the primary responsibility of the pastor? Preach the Word. Preach the Word with all the power and persuasiveness our personality and gifts allow. Preach the Word with clarity. Preach the Word with conviction. God's call demands it. God's people desire it. The world for whom Christ died needs it. Let's commit ourselves to do it—preach the Word!

"Challenge us to be more godly." Our culture pushes us toward attitudes, values, and beliefs that are sub-Christian, if not anti-Christian. Television is particularly adept at pushing an anti-Christian perspective. With such influences polluting our value systems, it is understandable why church members who were surveyed say they want to be challenged to godly living. "Help us to maintain a sense of right and wrong, a sense of good and bad in a world that has lost its moral underpinnings," they plead. Worship services that maintain solid footing on the unchanging Word of God can do that. As people are confronted with challenges to Christian beliefs and values, we offer stability in an unstable world. As Paul challenges us to remember, "But thanks be to God, who always leads us in triumphal procession in Christ and through us spreads everywhere the fragrance of the knowledge of him. For we are to God the aroma of Christ among those who are being saved and those who are perishing. To the one we are the smell of death; to the other, the fragrance of life. And who is equal to such a task?" (2 Cor. 2:14-16).

"Help us feel love and support of the church family." While some may believe that people attend worship services solely to praise God, most understand that worshipers need support and loving friendships. There remains the fact that God has created us as relational beings. Since we need each other, people come to worship needing to be with others and to feel their loving support. While worship primarily focuses on the vertical God-dimension of life, survey respondents remind us there is also a horizontal dimension, a need for genuine fellowship among God's people.

Can public worship (by nature a God-centered and corporate endeavor), encourage personal caring and intimacy? First, let's admit that worship services alone fall short of causing most people to feel warmly loved and accepted. Assimilation of newcomers occurs more readily when people feel bonded to persons in a more intimate way than worship services alone allow.

Two kinds of churches exist. In a "Teflon church" new attenders choose to "slide right on through." There's little to hold people. A church that depends solely on worship services to attract and hold newcomers is a Teflon church. A second kind of congregation can be described as a "Velcro church"—a place where people stick.[13] There is an attractive "stickability" that causes people to come back and stay. It is nearly impossible to create a "Velcro church" on worship services alone. By their corporate nature, worship services are less personal than are smaller groups—they don't promote the bonding and intimacy needed to cause people to stick. (How could they, when worshipers see only the back of the head of the person seated in the next pew?) Therefore, small-group ministry (perhaps the Sunday School) must give people an intimate, personal place to belong. Some church growth experts talk in terms of "celebration" (the Body of Christ in worship) and "cells," the larger group broken into more intimate, personal caring units of loving concern.

Recognizing the necessity of other ministries in addition to worship services, the question still remains: "How can leaders help worshipers feel the love and support of the church family in the services of worship?" Another way to ask this question is "How can worship services, even large ones, be made to feel more personal?" Let's quickly touch on two possibilities.

Create an Environment of Loving Acceptance

The way people feel about whether they are loved and accepted will depend as much on the people before and after the service as on what occurs during the service. "The atmosphere of warmth and acceptance is expressed most effectively by people who hold no official position. That's because the most gratifying welcome a visitor can receive is from someone he wouldn't expect to welcome him, in a place he didn't expect it to happen. It may be a warm comment by the person in the next pew. It might be several smiles and a lot of eye contact in the foyer before the service . . . Welcoming isn't just something done at the door; it's something *everyone* does all over the building."[14]

While those interactions cannot be programmed or controlled, certain things can be done to communicate the message "You are loved here." Enthusiastic greeters can initiate the coming-together of the pieces of the "welcoming puzzle." But those in official welcoming positions are only a catalyst to help create an atmosphere of loving acceptance. An environment of loving acceptance provides a positive first and continuing impression.

Practice Preservice Availability

While worshipers themselves communicate much about the warmth (or coldness) of the services to those attending, the pastor and staff can offer a personal touch even in a larger congregation. One way a pastor might do this is to circulate through the congregation before the service, briefly visiting with worshipers. In the minutes prior to the start of a service, a pastor can help move the emotional thermostat of the congregation toward "warm and loving." By practicing personal and caring attentiveness, the pastor begins to influence the emotional tone of the entire body. Obviously, plans for the service just ahead must be completed in advance to free this time for the pastor. It may be necessary to delegate to others the finishing of last-minute details. That early preparation is worth the effort!

Conclusion

What's really important in worship? Listening to those who spoke through the survey, five key areas are obvious.

They say, (1) Keep the services centered on God; (2) give us opportunity to express thanks to God; (3) let us hear God's Word; (4) challenge us to be more godly; and (5) help us feel the love and support of the church family.

Isn't the wisdom of these responses fascinating? There's nothing in their list that is unacceptable or contrary to God-honoring worship. It appears that these people almost instinctively know and want worship that has integrity and wholeness. "Lead us in a way that centers us on God and calls us to be His people," they say. As worship leaders, we will do well to heed their challenge.

5

What's Happening Around Us? Considering Our Culture

A 30-MINUTE DRIVE DOWN THE HIGHWAY FROM us lies the village of Yoder, Kansas. It's an Amish community. When we pass through the little town, my kids sit up and stare in wonder at the different things we see. We pass black buggies pulled by horses traveling along the highway. At the houses, the characteristic unadorned, distinctive dress of these folks is obvious. Women and girls wear plain long dresses. Males dress in black slacks with plain white or maybe gray shirts. Married men wear beards. A drive through Yoder is always different.

Early Mennonites, from whom the Amish descended, believed they should live apart from the world around them. They tended to establish isolated rural communities separate from the rest of society. Yoder is one of those towns. But the Amish rejected more than just physical closeness to other people. They also detached themselves from culture in rejecting technological advances. The wide-eyed stares of my kids as we drive through Yoder is not from an interest that inspires them to want to be like the Amish. Rather, my kids see these folks as curiosities. In separating from the surrounding culture, the Amish differences prevent these people from speaking to the culture at all. It's no surprise that the number of Amish is shrinking.

An obvious lesson that comes from this is that if we want to touch mainstream society with the good news of Christ, we have to maintain contact with the surrounding culture. Understanding our culture is necessary because those who have ignored culture have no chance of impacting it. This leads us to ask an important related question.

Why Should Leaders of Worship Be Concerned About What's Happening in the Surrounding Culture?

Obviously, some separatists or isolationists argue we don't need to concern ourselves about the surrounding culture. Since worship is for the "already committed," they would argue, culture should have no influence in the Church's worship. We must not allow the worship of God "to be squeezed into the world's own mold," they rightly insist. The Amish community is one example of those who discount the importance of cultural sensitivity.

Many others, however, believe it is essential to know what's happening around us. Missions strategists for years have advocated presenting the gospel in a form that can be appreciated by the local culture. One missiologist likens the gospel to a gift with the peculiar cultural habits and patterns being the packaging. He challenges missionaries to know the content of the gospel thoroughly but not become committed to the style or design of the wrapping that is learned from the culture. "To present that content in packaging that will be understood by the hearer is absolutely essential and requires a knowledge of his culture."[1]

Here are four more good reasons to be aware of our surrounding culture:

1. We need to know what our culture is like because the people we lead face the pressures of conforming to the culture's standards.

Those who worship in our services work, live, and play in a pressurized world that's increasingly hostile to the gospel of Jesus Christ. Unless we understand the world they inhabit, we will be unable to offer them the informed help they need to live effective Christian lives. Of particular importance is understanding the world our children and teens inhabit. Older Christians have probably already developed a worldview that allows them to cope with external pressures that are sub- or anti-Christian. But our children, teens, and even newer believers walk head-on into opposition without the benefit of a Christian worldview to guide them. Without Christian leaders who offer realistic responses to their real-world problems, our younger Christians will find solutions for themselves—solutions uninformed by Christianity and influenced more by the world than by God.

2. We need to know what our culture is like because understanding our society will enable us to communicate the truths of God more effectively.

Having grown up in the United States, I once assumed that I understood our culture. And to some degree I do. Yet in another way I don't understand it at all. Although I grew up in the United States, I also spent most of my years in the microcosm of the Church. (I see the Church as distinct from the world. If the Church really is God's called-out people, it must be distinctively different from the surrounding world.) The positive influence of the Church on my life has led me to view life very different from those in the world around me. Yet if I am to effectively communicate with people outside the Church, I need to know how they see life and what they think. We cannot hope to communicate the gospel if we ignore the cultural factor.

3. We need to know what our culture is like because in identifying those patterns that shape contemporary society, we can better avoid being unknowingly infected by it.

The Church can't be viewed as an island isolated from the rest of society. It cannot be isolated. As the culture changes, the Church changes. No doubt the Church is far different today than it was 40 years ago. Some persuasively argue that the Church is being shaped by the world more than it is shaping our culture. They may be right. But unless our leaders understand the pressures our culture exerts, we will in the future be stuffed even more into the world's mold than we have been in the past. By knowing the cultural patterns of our society, we can more effectively avoid being misshapen by it.

4. We need to know what our culture is like because we sometimes have to prophetically confront "what is" if we are to lead people to be what God desires.

The Old Testament prophet Jeremiah knew the culture he inhabited was not pleasing to God. His 40-year ministry to Judah was in many ways frustrating and an apparent failure. He confronted evil and the sins of the society only to be ignored or persecuted. Yet he was faithful to his calling. We would do well to remember his bold but unpopular words to Judah: "'Your wickedness will punish you; your backsliding will rebuke you. Consider then and realize how evil and bitter it is for you when you forsake the LORD your God and have no awe of me,' declares the Lord, the LORD Almighty" (Jer. 2:19). Like Jeremiah, only by understanding the society in which we live can we effectively confront that which displeases God and show His better way to live—whether people choose to listen or not.

Since these reasons challenge us as leaders of worship to better understand our culture, let's consider some key characteristics that profile contemporary American culture today.

What Values and Patterns Shape Our Contemporary Society?

The following characteristics profile contemporary, white, middle-class American culture. As such, the profile is admittedly limited. Certainly there are other groups we could discuss. And there are other characteristics we could cite. As we identify characteristics that profile this subculture, notice that many of the values seem to overlap. They seem to flow one into another. The profile should help us better understand how some people in our society make sense of their lives, how they think, and how their ideas relate to their actions. By understanding how people outside the walls of the church think and act, we should be better prepared to lead our people effectively in God-honoring worship.

People in our culture are more attuned to talk about "me" than "we." Remember sitting in front of the television watching the adventures of *The Lone Ranger?* The masked man and his sidekick friend, Tonto, were out to avenge wrong and be sure that justice was done. The image of a strong, quiet loner working for good is a part of our cultural mind-set. *The Lone Ranger* was a hit television show in part because the image of one who achieved good, largely without the help of others, is at the heart of the American mind.

> We believe in the dignity, indeed the sacredness, of the individual. Anything that would violate our right to think for ourselves, judge for ourselves, make our own decisions, live our lives as we see fit, is not only morally wrong—it is sacrilegious. Our highest and noblest aspirations, not only for ourselves, but for those we care about, for our society and for the world, are closely linked to our individualism. Yet, . . . some of our deepest problems both as individuals and as a society are also closely linked to our individualism. [For Americans to abandon] individualism would mean for us to abandon our deepest identity.[2]

This sometimes extreme focus on the self touches people's lives from all angles. Our radical individualism touches virtually every area of life—love, work, sex, child-rearing, and politics. It is notable that even in the way Americans view their faith, individualism reigns as a controlling norm. A Gallup poll showed 80 percent of Americans agreed that "an individual should arrive at his or her own religious beliefs independent of any churches or synagogues."[3] Gallup concludes, "Americans . . . increasingly view their faith as a matter between them and God, to be aided, but not necessarily influenced, by religious institutions."[4]

While American society once functioned more from the perspective of togetherness and mutual commitment, this is certainly not the case today. If contemporary America is to be understood, it must be seen as a nation where individualism rules.

What impact does individualism have on persons who come together to worship? When individualistic worshipers assemble, it is nearly impossible to create the vital interconnectedness that God wants to see in His Church. It's as if we see ourselves today as a big bag of marbles. If the bag is accidentally knocked over or kicked, we spill out in every direction. Some may well be lost. Nothing, except the bag, ties us together. But the connectedness and community that God desires in the church is more akin to a bunch of grapes than a bag of marbles. Grapes, being all tied together, won't roll off in every direction. They're not easily lost or separated. A common vine holds them together. Grapes, interconnected and interdependent, are a better picture of what God wants to see in the relationships that form as we assemble to glorify Him. Seeing worship purely as an individual experience where *I* get *my* needs met denies the community God wants to create.

People in our culture don't like to be told what to do. We'd rather assert our rights and enjoy our freedom. Yet we have little if any corresponding commitment to responsibility. We resist rules and don't like anybody telling us what to do. American individualism is closely related to our commitment to freedom. America, from its foundational roots, is about being free. Freedom is perhaps the most resounding, deeply held American value. In some ways it defines the good in our way of life. Yet, in American culture, freedom has come to mean more than the absence of unjust political tyranny. For many Americans freedom means "Nobody can tell me what to do." Often freedom is equated with freedom from responsibility and from community.

Our love of freedom is seen even in the way we relate to marriage. In today's society some see marriage as a prison or a cage that inhibits their personal growth and freedom. As a result, starting in the 1960s and continuing to the present, many persons who are unhappily married abandon their marriage commitments in the name of personal freedom. One proponent of this perspective states, "No longer need a person carry the burden of a single identity from the cradle to the grave. He is free to change lives and wives as often as he has the energy."[5] For many, changing marriages is not much more difficult than changing channels on television.

Our love of freedom without a commitment to responsibility also carries over into the arena of faith. "Americans . . . take a very independent approach to religion. . . . It must reflect the values of freedom that they assume in their daily social and political lives."[6] In the minds of many, the purpose of religion is to underwrite presently held beliefs and attitudes, rather than to challenge them and to offer new patterns of thought and action. Rather than thinking of religious faith as that which shapes life, many Americans use their faith as a psychological Band-Aid. This brand of faith does nothing to heal but only hides our wounds.

So for many Americans "freedom turns out to mean being left alone by others, not having other people's values, ideas, or styles of life forced upon [them], being free of arbitrary authority in work, family, and political life."[7]

The Scriptures speak of freedom in terms of deliverance, redemption, and freedom itself. But Christian freedom is primarily freedom from enslavement to sin. The deliverance from sin that God achieved in Christ Jesus is the basis of human freedom toward God. What must be realized (and what is not true in the American culture that worships freedom) is that we exercise freedom correctly when it is used to give ourselves back to God and to serve our neighbor in love. We are set free so that we can submit to God, set free to love Him with our whole heart and to love our neighbor as ourselves. The freedom that God gives lasts, is fulfilling, but it is responsible freedom. Paul admonishes the church at Rome, "Therefore, I urge you, brothers, in view of God's mercy, to offer your bodies as living sacrifices, holy and pleasing to God—this is your spiritual act of worship" (Rom. 12:1).

People in our culture prefer to "pull themselves up by their own bootstraps." I stood by my friend as he lay in an intensive care unit pondering his future. He was rushed to the trauma center soon after his pickup hit ice and flipped three times. Surgeons vigorously worked for hours to put the broken pieces of his body back together. During surgery his survival was uncertain.

In many ways my friend was the epitome of the American dream. Starting with nothing, he had dreamed, worked, and thought his way to great success in the building profession. Deeply committed to Christ, he lay there immobilized in traction, his back now screwed together by surgically implanted steel rods, his knee nearly destroyed by the accident. His words are hard for me to forget. "Always before," he lamented, "I've been able to work and think myself out of every situation. This time it's different—I can't."

Deep frustration oozed from him as he realized there was little he could do now to help himself. An inner voice told him he was supposed to take charge, to make his own way, take care of himself, and control the situation. That's the spirit of self-reliance—an integral part of American culture.

Pick up any newspaper and you'll likely read about welfare reform. CBS News reports that 96 percent of Americans believe fundamental reform of the welfare system is needed.[8] (That outstanding number may be the closest thing to consensus in America today.) A strong cultural belief is that we really should make our own way, especially financially. We hold dear the belief that the honest effort to get ahead should be rewarded, while those who sit idly by should not expect others to take care of them. We are a self-reliant people.

This notion of self-reliance even makes it hard for many to turn to God for help. According to a survey conducted for the Christian Broadcasting Network, the culture is "more likely to believe that man's reason and intellect, based on his learning and experience, rather than traditional religious values, are responsible for the advancement of mankind."[9] We should be able to learn, think, and work our way out of the difficulties and problems we encounter. This is part of the reason we talk so much about improving our education system. Inwardly we believe that if we can just know enough and work hard enough, *if we will really try,* we can succeed.

The demographics of self-reliance reveal interesting patterns. Gallup's findings regarding American self-reliance can be summarized in four statements: (1) males tend to be more self-reliant than females; (2) younger adults are generally more self-reliant than older persons; (3) those with some college education tend to depend more on themselves; and (4) Roman Catholics and nonevangelicals tend to rely more on themselves than do evangelicals.[10]

People in our society are driven by the god of success. A youngster defined success as "having whatever you want, whenever you want it." Too often we measure success by what we own. Our culture promotes the acquisition of a house, and then a bigger one. We are encouraged to buy newer, more expensive cars with more and more extras. Rapidly changing styles call us to replace clothes long before they are worn out. But the problem is not simply cultural—it is a problem of the human heart.

Ron Blue recounted his experience in Africa a few years back. He visited an African pastor who lived in a thatched-roof hut made of cow manure. Blue asked the pastor an important question: "Can you tell me the biggest barrier to the spread of the gospel in this part of the world?"

His host responded quickly, "Oh, yes. That's easy—*materialism.*"

Blue was surprised. He suspected that in this primitive setting poor communication, difficult transportation, or a host of other problems would have been the answer he received. So he challenged the pastor's response: "What do you mean, materialism? These people have next to nothing."

The pastor explained: "Well, if a man has a mud hut, he wants a cow manure hut. If he has a cow manure hut, he wants a stone hut. If he has a thatched roof, he wants a tin roof. If he has one acre, he wants two. Materialism is a disease of the heart. It has nothing to do with where you live."[11]

While striving for success measured by what we own is not unique to Americans, we have elevated striving for success measured by the "stuff" we own to an art form. In 1961 sociologist Peter L. Berger evaluated American culture with the observation that one of the most commonly held American values is that of success competitively achieved.[12] Yet the disease of materialism keeps growing. Merton Strommen says, "Fifteen years ago, the number one goal of college freshman was 'developing a meaningful philosophy of life'; today it has switched to 'making money.' . . . Those most motivated by making money has grown from 30% to 70%."[13]

Americans see life as a race. In every race some win, others lose, and most are bunched in the middle. The predominant goal today is to be the winner. For Americans, winning is measured in a most specific manner. In our competitive, achievement-oriented society, we measure success by how much money we have and how much stuff we accumulate. A bumper sticker explains the national mind-set: "The one with the biggest pile of stuff wins."

Another measure of success for Americans is progress, especially progress at work. And progress at work results in upward mobility. But making it to the next tier is not enough, for there are always higher levels to attain. Thus, the achievement of success provides only a short-lived satisfaction. It tends to produce people who are driven and unable to enjoy their daily existence. Americans want to be the star, uniquely successful and admired. We want to stand out from the crowd of ordinary folks who don't know how to succeed.[14] Those who attain a measure of success are often surprised to discover that their success elicits not the admiration and approval for which they hoped, but rather jealousy and envy from those yet to attain the goal. Yet many Americans are not satisfied to be near the top; they drive forward to be alone at the top, to be king of the hill. One person observed, "The only trouble with the formula for success is that it is the same as the formula for a nervous breakdown."

Americans today have lost sight of life's ultimate purpose. It is important to know why we do what we do. As a nation we have lost sight of why we exist. We no longer have a clear picture of what ultimately matters.

> For several centuries, we have been embarked on a great effort to increase our freedom, wealth, and power. For over 100 years, a large part of the American people, the middle class, has imagined that the virtual meaning of life lies in the acquisition of ever-increasing status, income, and authority, from which genuine freedom is supposed to come. Our achievements have been enormous. . . . Yet we seem to be hovering on the very brink of disaster, not only from international conflict but from the internal incoherence of our own society. . . . What has gone wrong?[15]

What's wrong is that many Americans sense that even if they achieve their goals, something essential is missing. Yet most often we fail to comprehend what contributes to emptiness and what is lacking.

Freedom, affluence, achievement, sexual involvement, ever-increasing possessions, high technology, and self-fulfillment techniques have proven inadequate as sources of real purpose. All fall woefully short, leaving those who pursue them unsatisfied and unfulfilled. As one person put it, "When you get to the top of the ladder of success, you discover it is leaning against the wrong building." James W. Fowler speaks of our need for meaning: "We do not live by bread alone, sex alone, success alone, and certainly not by instinct alone. We require meaning. We need purpose and priorities; we must have some grasp on the big picture."[16] Yet many Americans have lost their concept of what holds ultimate purpose and meaning for their lives. They are adrift, not knowing what matters ultimately.

Because we have lost sight of any significant purpose in life, many are searching. Having concluded that life has to be more than just a race to accumulate things and knowing the pain of broken relationships, many are searching for a cause.

Our society today is morally adrift. A nightly news program interviewed a young student who nearly graduated from Yale. Two months prior to receiving his degree, he was discovered to have submitted a fraudulent entrance application. His deception included a forged transcript that turned his C average into straight A's.[17] Two letters of reference were submitted from nonexistent faculty members. Another letter from a college administrator was forged. The student gained entrance to the prestigious university deceptively and faced possible charges of grand larceny since he had accepted more than $60,000 in academic aid based on the bogus application.

The greatest tragedy was not in the student's intentional deception. The greater tragedy came in a television interview of the now-expelled student, in which he displayed absolutely no remorse or sorrow for his deceptive application. Rather, he was disturbed that the university would try to hold him accountable for his deception. Since he had completed much of the work for his degree, he believed he should be allowed to graduate and that "as an American citizen" he was entitled to the money, despite his deceptive application. He seemed totally shocked by the suggestion that he could go to jail for his crime. He was prepared to get ahead at all costs.

Once America shared a set of commonly agreed-upon standards of behavior and ethics. We believed together that some things (like telling the truth) were right, and others, (like falsifying applications) were wrong. Today we have no such set of mutually agreed-upon truths. Moral relativism has replaced any commonly shared system of values in our society.

What has happened to our ethics has been described by the word "relativism." Relativism is a discounting or outright denial of moral absolutes. It asserts the impossibility of knowing what is right and wrong. Not only is the possibility of knowing absolute moral truth discounted, but also some say that anyone who claims to know right from wrong should be feared.

Allan Bloom asserts, "There is one thing a professor can be absolutely certain of: almost every student entering the university believes, or says he believes, that truth is relative. . . . [While they may come from diverse backgrounds and perspectives] they are unified only in their relativism." Bloom says today's students are taught to fear as dangerous those who profess the ability to know truth. "Relativism is necessary to openness, and this is the virtue, the only virtue, which all primary education for more than 50 years has dedicated itself to inculcating."[18]

What replaces moral absolutes? The answer is clear: "Even the deepest ethical virtues are justified as matters of personal preference."[19] The reign of self replaces the rule of truth. "What is right" comes to be understood as "what is right for me," or for that matter, "what is right for you." *I'm OK—You're OK*, a pop psychology book, suggests that judging others, or even oneself, is wrong. Both mutual acceptance and self-acceptance are the controlling values that should guide society, the relativists would say.

If America no longer believes in traditional morality, what shall be done with the "absolutes" that still reside, at least in the memories of some Americans? How is the denial of moral certitude justified? It appears that moral relativism is validated from three perspectives. First, when making moral decisions, there is a trend to replace traditional religion with personal conscience. In a *McCall's* magazine readers' survey, "Of 18,000 respondents, 55% claimed to be 'born again.' . . . Yet most said they relied primarily on their own consciences rather than the traditions of their religions to make moral decisions. Less than 3% said they would go to a clergyman for guidance."[20]

A second way of substantiating relativism is to jump on the bandwagon of tolerance and moral diversity. In our pluralistic society, mutual tolerance is simply the expected norm. Even many evangelical Christians are jumping on the bandwagon by adopting universal acceptance and compassion, along with a heightened tolerance of relativism and diversity as key values.[21] In this matter we are adopting the perspective of the culture around us.

The third and perhaps most deceptive tactic used to justify moral relativism is the trend to define every decision by using the language of sociology or psychology, not the language of religion, ethics, or morality. Instead of calling murder a sin, we question what societal pressures made a person stab his or her mother. Instead of seeing the murderer as a criminal, the accused is viewed as a "victim of society." Rather than judging individuals guilty of criminal behavior, we parade a host of psychologists to the stand to convince the court that the actions were the result of some psychological maladjustment for which the defendant is not responsible. The "politically correct" position is to use the views and nonjudgmental standards of the social sciences for analyzing each situation.

In clear distinction, the Willowbank Report of the Lausanne Conference on World Evangelism affirms, "The Gospel . . . evaluates all cultures according to its own criteria of truth and righteousness, and insists on moral absolutes in every culture. We wish to . . . emphasize that even in this present age of relativity moral absolutes remain."[22] In an age where uncertainty is praised and certitude ridiculed, Christ still provides truth on which we can depend.

American culture increasingly embraces religious pluralism. Not so long ago, Christians feared America would become atheistic. Instead of rejecting the concept of God, however, as a nation we have come to embrace many gods. Having no commonly agreed-upon truths that guide our faith, American culture is becoming increasingly religiously pluralistic. The *Yearbook of American and Canadian Churches 1992* identifies 224 religious bodies functioning in the United States. The editors say many more have not been included.[23] George Gallup similarly observes the religious diversity in America seen in the hundreds of denominations in the country.[24] Closely tied to American independence and individualism, pluralism is a celebration of individual choice; not only are persons allowed to be different, but they are *encouraged* to be different. Alternative lifestyles are celebrated and considered the "politically correct" norm. Intolerance is ridiculed as close-minded, judgmental bigotry. One writer says the typical unchurched person in our society prides himself in his tolerance but sees Christians as narrow-minded.[25]

Is religious tolerance a soon-to-pass fad or a growing phenomenon? We can point to a time in the history of this country when religious pluralism was all but absent. The religion of America before the Civil War was almost uniformly Christian. Unity in shared beliefs, not diversity, was the norm. Even as recently as the 1950s, sociologist Will Herzberg could write *Protestant, Catholic, Jew,* in which he described the dominant American religious groups. However, no such unity is present today. America today is far more pluralistic than it was in the 1950s. Where is the nation headed with respect to religious pluralism? George Gallup says our growing pluralism in America reflects a movement away from agreement on any religious view. We are becoming less of a white Anglo-Saxon Protestant nation and a somewhat less Judeo-Christian nation."[26] The trend will continue.

This predicted pattern is related to the age composition of the contemporary population. The great numbers of baby boomers is a key factor. "Though the baby boom is no monolith, it is united in its tolerance of diversity. The educational level of the baby boom makes it more accepting and even encouraging of individual differences and alternative lifestyles. The result is an increasingly diverse American culture."[27]

In our society, our lives are increasingly compartmentalized. In 1994 Aldridge Ames became the worst nightmare of the Central Intelligence Agency (CIA). Ames, a CIA employee for 31 years, revealed to the Soviets many secrets that breached the security of our nation. He was convicted of being a double spy who directly caused the death of at least four Soviets who secretly worked for the United States. Upon conviction, Ames was sentenced to life in prison.

In an interview, Ames was asked how he could do such a despicable thing as selling out his fellow workers and his country. Ames rationalized his actions by saying, "I tend to put some of these things in separate boxes [in my mind], and compartment feelings and thoughts." His dual existence, Ames said, long ago forced him to "compartment" his mind.[28]

Aldridge Ames is not alone in compartmentalized living. When examining American culture, compartmentalized lives become frequently evident. The nation's willingness to think in terms of segmented lives is seen in recent political campaigns. It has become common for the media to do character checks on the candidates. The backgrounds of those offering themselves for public service are carefully scrutinized. However, even if the media uncovers unsavory details from a candidate's life, it is not unusual for the candidate to respond by saying, "What I do in private is no one else's business." While American citizens frequently insist that candidates tell the truth about their private lives, many of them seem to believe that what is done in private has little influence on what will be done in the public arena.

Marion Barry, mayor of Washington, D.C., is a prime example. While serving as mayor, Barry was caught on video in the act of using crack cocaine. Yet after he went through a period of rehabilitation, the citizens of our nation's capital re-elected Barry—even following his embarrassing exposure. Many Americans seem comfortable with compartmentalizing life into public and private spheres.

Compartmentalizing life also touches the way we view our public and private lives. The desire to separate our public world from our private life results in a phenomena called "cocooning." Cocooning describes how people arrive home from work, push a button on their garage door opener, drive into their home's attached garage, shut the door, and become invisible. If they venture outside at all, it's behind their backyard privacy fence. The home becomes the center of life's private activities and relationships. But it is done as much as possible in isolation from people and from other segments of life. Cocooning secludes the home and the family from the rest of life. The home becomes our castle, where we expect to be safe and alone. At home, persons escape the pressures of public life. The isolated family provides an island of security and separation in a pressure-packed sea of public existence.

Along with the family-home compartmentalization, religion comprises one of life's private sectors. "Religion is relegated pretty exclusively to private life."[29] And because Americans are adept at compartmentalizing their lives, religion often has relatively little influence on other aspects of daily existence. In America, religion does more to reinforce preconceived notions than it does to challenge already-held assumptions.[30] Perhaps Americans turn to religion to get through times of stress and struggle. But instead of allowing religion to transform them, many Americans use their faith only to meet their felt needs. In any case, Americans largely regard religion as a component of their private lives.

How does a compartmentalized-privatized view of life impact Americans? Three results deserve mention. First, we learn how to be both religious and secular at the same time. Americans can view themselves as spiritual even if their lives show little evidence of religious influence.

Second, while many Americans have attempted to make their faith personal and private, they often feel very empty. It is simply not possible to turn the gospel of Jesus Christ successfully into a self-serving, private faith that relieves personal stress without committing ourselves to discipline and social engagement. Attempts to reduce the gospel to selfish ends distorts the righteous purposes for which Christ came into the world. If our society tries to use the gospel for mere pragmatic interests, the end will be one of disillusionment and frustration.

The third result of compartmentalization and privatization is hardly surprising. Studies show that as many as 4 in 10 Americans confess periods of intense loneliness. We are among the loneliest people in the world.[31] By withdrawing from public life into isolated enclaves within the family, Americans have found that the separation from others can be lonely. The prevalence of compartmentalized and privatized lives does not appear to serve American society well.

Americans are intensely interested in "what works." The culture of the United States is also characterized by a deep concern for what works. The dominant question is not "What is right?" but rather "What achieves results?"

Ted Oster exemplifies the typical American spirit. "I guess I'm pretty result-oriented," he says, "and whatever produces a good result must be right, and whatever produces a bad result must be wrong."[32] Acts, then, according to this belief system, are not right or wrong in themselves. The criteria used for determining acceptability of any action is the result produced. It is easy to believe "the end justifies the means."

Pragmatism is carried into nearly every area of life. It is sometimes positively applied. Approaching education pragmatically helps Americans seek to learn how students can better learn. Time-saving conveniences abound, since Americans concern themselves with finding a better way. But sometimes pragmatism becomes a controlling norm that damages society. Examples include marriage and religion. On marriage, a typical reason cited for continuing a marriage is not commitment, love, or fidelity, but rather the fact that the relationship works. Conversely, if the marriage does not work, we discard it and get one that does.

Likewise, religion is often judged pragmatically. Predominantly in American culture, folks are interested in faith principally to the extent that it meets their own personal needs. "It works for me," Americans would be apt to say. Pragmatism, not the holiness of God, acts as the controlling norm of religion.

The key question asked of religion by many is not, "Is Christianity true?" Rather, they ask, "Does Christianity work?"

In spite of severe societal problems, people in our culture are optimistic. It has been my practice, whenever I'm not in my own church, to visit various Protestant evangelical churches across the nation. As I've said, in my travels I have observed that few American Protestant evangelical pastors lead their people to confession of sin and subsequent repentance. Many services never mention sin at all. An attitude saying "We're all OK" pervades many services. We seem to have difficulty dealing with anything that is not encouraging and upbeat. This unhealthy and unfounded optimism of the human condition has potentially tragic spiritual consequences. To ignore sin does not make it go away.

Yet our national culture is temperamentally optimistic. Americans have a can-do attitude that tends to think problems can be fixed and fixed now. Such optimism may cause Americans to miss the fact that some long-standing problems may not have quick-fix solutions. This same optimism leaves Americans vulnerable to politicians who will tell them what they want to hear in order to get elected. While the culture applauds optimism and the power of positive thinking, some believe Americans have taken the trait too far. At least one sociologist says unfounded optimism may be America's chief mental disease.[33]

Conclusion

These 10 profile elements could be augmented by others. We could discuss the disintegration of the nuclear family and a restlessness that is never satisfied. Such restless persons seem to think they must always move on to the next stage in their life or the next adventure. Additional topics could include the rise of women to leadership positions, the graying of America, and the decline in work ethic.

The 10 characteristics of American culture call for those who lead in worship to be firmly committed to God and the truths revealed in His Word. We are called to be *thermostats* that change our environment, not merely *thermometers* that measure it. While we must be sensitive to what is happening in our culture, there is always the risk that sensitivity means we will allow the society to mold us. It is not acceptable for us simply to condone and accept societal traits that run counter to the godly principles established in Scripture and set forth by Jesus Christ. The informed and faithful worship leader not only should be aware of these cultural characteristics but also must evaluate them in light of theology. It is our responsibility to point worshipers to God's "better way."

6

Facing the Music: Choosing Your Worship Style

BOTH THE CHURCH AND OUR SOCIETY ARE BUZZ-ing about the changes in worship taking place today. Along with many books and articles that focus on how the Church should worship, Peter Jennings examined the issue in an hour-long ABC special report titled "In the Name of God."[1] The style of worship used in services designed to glorify God is a hot topic today—and one that's very controversial. The controversial nature of the issue was emphasized when one person observed that the first murder in history occurred after a disagreement over worship styles. Key questions in the controversy abound. Can churches that feature *traditional* services survive and thrive in the coming decade? Or will services have to be reoriented to more *contemporary* tastes? What about the heritage and power of *liturgical* patterns of worship? Will services need to be redesigned as seeker-sensitive, or should worship target the already-committed? These and many other questions lay behind the concerns surrounding the worship styles we use today.

In this chapter we'll try to better understand how we've arrived at a time when traditional styles of worship are under criticism, if not attack. What's behind all the changes in worship? We'll also touch on the key role of music in worship—whatever style is employed. An examination of three styles of worship, currently popular in evangelical Protestantism, will finally lead us to suggest several important questions to ask before attempting to implement changes in the style of worship of the church you lead.

What's Behind All the Worship Changes?

A key area of controversy and concern in the discussion among both laity and clergy concerns worship styles. Recent issues of one denomination's newsletter to pastors contained ongoing debate on what is appropriate in contemporary patterns of worship. Should we return to more liturgical patterns to enable our people to truly worship? Are traditional patterns to be retained, resisting any changes at all? Or should more contemporary patterns that speak to younger people be adopted? Strong feelings exist on all sides of the controversy. Complicating the debate is a strong pragmatic concern. Pastors are concerned with "what's working" in worship innovation. Often "what's working" means what draws new people into the church's services.

The debate is not solely the concern of clergy types. Within just a few days of my writing this, a concerned group of Christian sociologists will convene a multiday conference. The sole topic of discussion—"changing worship styles." Obviously, current styles of worship concern the Church and the nation today.

What factors have led to the current upheaval and concern about worship styles? It's often tempting to explain complex developments with uncomplicated answers. But current developments in changing worship styles cannot be adequately explained with simplistic answers. Many factors converge to generate the current controversy and concern about worship styles. While any explanation of what has led to the current state of worship will risk oversimplification and perhaps overlook important factors, several elements involved in leading us to our present status can be identified. Let's consider five of these factors:

1. As a nation, we are increasingly consumer-minded. More than ever, Americans today respond as consumers. "Americans consume everything from groceries to clothing to furniture to cars to entertainment. Consumerism is evident in television commercials, newspaper ads, and the public relations segment of the business world. Consumerism is the engine that drives American society, and it is the driving force guiding them as they choose their churches."[2] When the time comes to choose a place of worship, people bring their deeply ingrained consumer-mindedness along. In other words, Americans today demand more choices in worship than they did in former days. The typical choice offered by the church in the past, "Take it or leave it," no longer suffices when worshipers come with strong consumer-minded tendencies.

Elmer Towns explains consumerism's impact on worship, "As consumers, . . . Americans go where they feel comfortable with the style of worship that best reflects their inclinations and temperament."[3] Churches concerned with reaching persons not currently attending worship must face the reality that providing alternative worship styles is one frequently effective way to attract new attenders.

2. Americans are today less concerned about doctrine, name, or denominational affiliation. A second factor involved in changing worship styles involves the differences between past and present patterns of choosing a place of worship. Historically, most Americans chose their church based on (1) doctrine, (2) name, or (3) denomination.[4] Worship styles were hardly considered in the decision. Today, however, patterns have changed greatly. Contemporary Americans appear less concerned about what a church believes, about it being mainline, or about its denominational affiliation. Some churches in recognizing the contemporary mind-set even view denominational affiliation as a liability and choose to remove denominational identifiers, such as emblems or name, from their advertising.

Each morning as I drive to the office, I pass the campus of a large congregation. The modern facility belongs to one of Kansas's largest churches, named by Elmer Towns as one of America's "ten most innovative churches." The congregation, having grown rapidly in recent years, has more than 3,000 members and a weekly worship attendance in excess of 2,000. The name on their sign reads Central Community Church. There's not a denominational label in sight.

Central Community Church is one of a large number of "community churches" that populate the current American landscape. The mailbox today contained a direct-mail letter inviting us to attend a new church beginning in the northwest part of our city: you guessed it—Northwest Community Church. These generic, unaligned (at least in their advertising) congregations testify to the nondenominational mind-set in America today. It's a different world!

If people today no longer select a church primarily on the basis of doctrine, name, or denomination, what factors most significantly influence their decision? One study reveals that the three most important factors involved in people's choice of a church today are (1) the style of worship, (2) the quality of ministry, and (3) beliefs that directly influence lifestyle.[5] Notice the primary importance of the style of worship. A factor once not even in the top three has sprung to the top of the list. Although by no means is the style of worship the only pertinent factor, it is for Americans currently the *most important* factor involved in choosing a new church home.

When we tie this fact together with the realization that "Modern American culture places great emphasis on self, independence, and personal fulfillment," we come to see that when people choose a place of worship today, they want services that touch their feelings.[6] These issues fuel the current controversy over emotion-centered contemporary styles of worship.

Another factor involved in the discussion over worship styles is that . . .

3. People today have a broader exposure to various worship styles through television. Television touches contemporary life in many ways, and one is in exposing us to differing styles and patterns than we may have otherwise experienced. For those who once were born into, grew up in, and attended only one church, there was little awareness of how others worshiped. When other patterns were experienced, those styles may have appeared strange or odd. Long-instilled habits and traditions in worship often caused differing patterns simply to be rejected.

However, television now makes it possible for people who are already less committed to traditional patterns of worship to experience the ways others do it. And when they see how worship is done on television, they often see large churches whose very size gives the ability to present high-quality worship celebrations that draw from deep pools of congregational (if not professional) talent. The combination of less commitment to past styles, a more mobile population, and an increased awareness of alternative worship styles causes people to be increasingly unwilling to accept without question whatever worship style the church happens to offer. Television has also contributed to the broadened awareness of alternative styles of worship.

4. Baby boomers, who once left the Church en masse, are returning to the Church, but without the commitment to traditional styles and patterns. In contemporary society, the first exposure most new people have to church is in public worship. First impressions often determine whether these newcomers choose to return. The corporate worship of the church becomes the bridge to all the other ministries of the congregation.

After many years of absence, many baby boomers are looking again in the direction of the Church. Their years of absence have left them unacquainted with, and uncommitted to, traditional music as well as the historic patterns of worship in the Church. Doug Murren speaks as a baby boomer himself: "Unless you're a boomer, you will find it hard to realize what a big leap it is for us to jump into traditional forms of worship and church that worked well before the 1960s."[7] Having grown up in a visually oriented world that is fast-paced and flowing, these persons anticipate and expect worship experiences that are high quality, practical, action-oriented, and less formal—very different from many traditional worship services.

While many characteristics of baby boomer mentality can be criticized, one trait that deserves commendation is their desire to participate. Baby boomers returning to the Church are less willing simply to "show up, pay up, and shut up." They demand to be vitally involved in congregational life, including the worship experience. Participation in worship is essential for these persons. No longer willing to "watch" worship, these people insist on experiencing their praise of God.

Robert Webber reports the following discussion with a friend who was upset with his own church's style of worship. "What offends you about the way worship is conducted in your church?" Webber asked.

The man responded, "It's the pastor-centered service. The pastor does everything—leads the service, reads the Scripture, prays, and preaches. What I want is a service where the gifts of all God's people are expressed."[8] Persons today expect to participate in the worship experience—not to simply show up to watch others worship.

5. Some churches, recognizing that traditional patterns of worship will probably not reach many of these adults, have been willing to try new approaches to worship. Right or wrong, healthy or sick, the above-mentioned factors place the Church in an awkward position. Either we allow a large segment of the population to stay away from organized religion, or we reshape our worship in a way that appeals to those who reject traditional styles. The desire to evangelize presently unreached segments of contemporary society fuels some of the changes in worship styles today.

Some have observed that the cultural shift comes primarily from outside the Church. There is little doubt that the Church is being influenced by surrounding culture—more than she is influencing it. While this is sadly the case, many contend that to win at least a hearing from contemporary American society will demand that the Church adopt styles and patterns of worship different from what has been offered in the past.

The Key Role of Music

A key to redesigning worship involves music. Choosing a worship style is largely a matter of music. And the type of music we use in worship establishes who we'll attract to that worship service. Rick Warren says, "Music is the most important factor in determining your evangelistic target, even more than preaching style. . . . When you choose your music, you are determining exactly who you are going to reach and who you are not going to reach. More than any other factor, tell me what the music is in a church, and I will tell you who that church will be able to reach and who they will never be able to reach."[9]

Music also drives people's emotional response to worship. It has been said that "music opens the heart so the Word can fill it." When the music chosen for the worship service touches the hearts of those attending, it is easier to communicate God's Word effectively through the sermon. Closely linked to the type of music used is the style of worship.

What Choices Present Themselves Today?

Before we look at several differing styles of worship, let's say up front that God ministers to different people and is himself glorified through various styles of worship. The style itself is probably unimportant to God if the heart motive of worshipers is right. Robert Webber asserts, "The biblical and historical process of worship does not necessitate a particular type of worship. . . . Nevertheless, some elements of biblical and historical worship—namely, the overall order and the underlying structure—ought to be found in every style of worship. The infrastructure of this order may vary from group to group as would the style, ranging from formal to informal."[10] We examined patterns of good worship in chapter 2.

As we look at three worship styles, the aim is not to endorse or belittle any particular style of worship. God speaks to some of His children through each style. I will try to fairly describe some characteristics of each style and comment on who might be most likely drawn to each of these styles. The following chart compares the three worship styles we will discuss: liturgical, traditional, and praise and worship.

Three Worship Styles Compared

Praise and Worship	Traditional	Liturgical
Emotion-centered	◄─────────────►	Intellect-centered
Person-oriented	Conversion-oriented	God-oriented
Spontaneous		Fixed
Prayer-focused	Sermon-centered	Scripture-focused

I will not attempt to examine every style of worship that exists. James F. White, worship historian, classifies Protestant worship in nine separate traditions.[11] (He uses the word "tradition" in the same way we talk of "styles.") Let's think together about three distinct styles commonly found in American Protestant evangelical worship.

Liturgical Worship

Liturgical worship has its roots firmly planted in history. Worshipers may sing the same hymns their grandparents sang decades ago. The order of service will likely be nearly identical each week. Liturgical worship has been described by some as "high church." Others call it formal or orthodox. In liturgical worship often a printed order of service includes the Lord's Prayer, the Doxology, choir anthems, and a responsive reading of Scripture. A choral response may conclude the pastoral prayer. The Gloria Patri ("Glory be to the Father, and to the Son, and to the Holy Ghost . . .") as well as the singing of "Amen" at the end of each hymn may characterize every service.

A liturgical service often employs classical music. Works of great composers like Bach or Handel may be prominent. Traditional hymns are often used. When worshipers enter, the music they hear will flow from the organ, the most prominent instrument in liturgical worship. The sanctuary where worship occurs will be a place of reverence. Reverence is a higher priority than relationships (at least in the sanctuary).

Since the core of liturgical worship appeals to the intellect, the prayers may be written and the order preset. Scripture lessons are selected from the lectionary suggestions of the day. The church calendar guides the service's theme. The attitude toward the service is guided by the instruction of 1 Cor. 14:40: "Let all things be done decently and in order" (KJV). One with a liturgical mind complained of his pastor's too-casual approach to prayer. "My wife makes a list before she goes shopping. You would think anyone would have the decency to think through what he wanted to say to God."[12] One who appreciates the order, thought, and dignity of liturgical worship might view prayer in worship this way.

Critics of liturgical worship complain of ritualism, dead orthodoxy, and coldness. They might protest the lack of emotional fervor and criticize thoughtless repetition of creeds, prayers, or Scripture. Critics probably believe that those drawn to liturgical worship don't really have a heartfelt commitment to God or a real desire to praise Him.

In spite of the critics, there are those who prefer liturgical worship. Who might most likely be drawn to a liturgical style? Liturgical worship appeals primarily to those who are more intellectually inclined. As such, liturgical worship through history has attracted the more educated and affluent segments of society. The "common person" has not often found liturgical style attractive. In liturgical worship, more emphasis is placed on the objective events of what God has done in Christ Jesus than on what my faith "means to me." Emotion is most often subordinated to objective truth.

Praise and Worship

If the watchword of liturgical worship is decency and order, the heartbeat of the praise and worship style is the conviction that "God inhabits the praise of His people." This style of worship is oriented toward feelings and flow. Being primarily person-centered, the emphasis falls on emotion instead of intellect. Where liturgical worship concentrates on the truth of Scripture, the praise and worship style emphasizes more the importance of prayer. Prayers are composed on the spot. Since the immediacy of God is highly valued, a prewritten prayer would be considered unspiritual. Spirit-led leadership must be able and willing to "go with the flow and sense the movement of events."[13]

Participation of the worshipers in the worship celebration is central to this style. Instead of being sung *to*, worshipers sing. Involvement is encouraged as the congregation stands through extended singing of choruses, as worshipers clap to the rhythm of the music and lift their hands in praise. The tone is almost always upbeat, the outlook positive, and the sentiment joyful. Prayer will abound, and many worshipers may voice their prayers aloud simultaneously. "The distinct contribution of praise and worship tradition/ charismatic worship is its openness to the Spirit," says Robert Webber.[14]

Flow in the service is important to the praise and worship style. Instead of singing a hymn, stopping, announcing another, and beginning again, the worship leader in this style guides the flow from one chorus to another. Contemporary choruses comprise the bulk of the musical menu. Instead of a choir, a worship team will probably support not a minister of music but a worship leader. The worship team's responsibility is not to sing *to* the congregation but to lead the congregation to *participate* in the worship experience. As such, the choruses chosen will probably be feeling-oriented. The primary musical instrument will likely be a synthesizer. Drums and guitars may accompany the electronic keyboard. The service may be built around a theme that guides the chorus selection and ties together with the sermon that follows.

Some outsiders might complain that after a while the music in these services begins to sound repetitious and unsettling. One individual describes his personal reaction to a praise and worship service: "I sensed the steady diet of choruses become tiring. There were spaces in the worship where I wanted a change of pace, more substance to my song, some quietness. I felt I was kept in a constant state of enthusiasm, that the continuous use of the same rhythm and same style of praise became somewhat trite, and that I simply wanted all the noise to stop for a while and give me a chance to be quiet before the Lord."[15]

Who most appreciates the praise and worship style? Early on, the praise and worship style "appealed almost entirely to the 'disinherited.'"[16] Yet, while originating with the lowest rungs of the social ladder, as is common among movements, over time the style began to gain respectability and is now accepted among all segments of society. Today, if we were to attend a praise and worship style service, we may well observe a congregation made up largely of persons age 50 and younger—baby boomers. Their dress may well be more casual than what might be found in services in other worship styles. These worshipers represent a large cross-section of the socioeconomic spectrum, from poor to rich, professional to laborer. The style is popular with many seeking to worship God in a heartfelt manner.

Traditional

From the outset it has been more difficult to describe traditional worship. It seems easier to describe other styles of worship in Protestantism than it does to characterize traditional worship. The term is itself loaded. In one respect, whatever style we ourselves have experienced is, for us, traditional. Here the term is used not just as a way of characterizing what I have personally known, but as a way to label middle-of-the-road Protestant American worship frequently experienced in a variety of denominational backgrounds.

The History Behind Traditional Worship

To gain insight into traditional worship, a quick look back into history is important. James F. White, in his book *Protestant Worship: Traditions in Transition,* tells us that traditional worship originated on the American frontier. (White actually labels this style frontier or frontier-revival worship. We call it traditional.) The American frontier presented a new and different situation. People were spread over vast geographical distances. Travel was difficult. Churches were few—clergy even fewer. Most people were not churchgoers.

So the problem confronting church leaders was not how to conduct good worship. Their problem was how to design services for the unchurched. How do you attract and convert to God those who are presently outside the influence of any church? (Does this problem sound at all familiar? It sounds much like the problem addressed by advocates of seeker-sensitive services.) In response to this problem, for perhaps the first time, services on the American frontier were designed with the primary aim of winning converts. Prior to this, worship services had aimed at the central task of glorifying God. Evangelistic services were held, but always outside the church and not in place of the worship time. But now in frontier worship the central purpose shifted.

The primary aim was no longer to worship but to win the lost. Evangelism became the heart of frontier services. James F. White observes, "Although several traditions practiced evangelistic preaching outside the church, none of them developed a whole system of worship that led *to* baptism rather than leading *from* it."[17] Frontier worship developed a whole system of worship leading to conversion of the lost to Christ.

The impact of the shift to an evangelistic focus was, and is, dramatic. The aim of the sermon became to convince the lost to turn to Christ. Services ended with an evangelistic appeal often known as an altar call. The camp meeting became an effective method used to bring widely scattered people together for the purpose of guiding them to God. What occurred is properly called "the Americanization of Protestant worship," for the impact of these changes spread far and wide, influencing how we worship in this country even today.[18] This background lies behind what is "the most prevalent worship tradition in American Protestantism (and maybe in American Christianity)."[19]

Characteristics of Traditional Worship

Enough of looking back. What are the characteristics of traditional worship today? In many ways, traditional worship represents a middle-of-the-road approach to worship. Traditional describes the worship of those Protestant congregations "whose worship is not quite as fixed as that of the liturgical church and not quite as free as those with a more extemporaneous style."[20] In traditional services the sermon is the centerpiece. In some situations the centrality of the sermon is so significant that the service is viewed as being composed of preliminaries and a sermon. The largest block of time is devoted to the sermon. A typical traditional order of worship may consist of two songs (probably a hymn and a gospel song), followed by prayer, a choir special, offering, another musical special, and the sermon, which concludes with an invitation to come to Christ. Announcements of congregational activities will be inserted into the service somewhere, although most worship leaders seem to struggle continually to know where they fit best.

In traditional worship, choruses and hymns may be used. But personal, testimony-oriented gospel songs are often more popular. The predominant musical instrument is the piano, perhaps accompanied by an organ. During key points of the service, worshipers may feel free to express vocally an "amen" or "hallelujah," although it seems this pattern is becoming less and less frequent.

The traditional approach to worship probably appeals most to those who have a long, or at least a former, experience in the church. Many traditional congregations are comprised mostly of persons more than 50 years of age who have grown up in church with this tradition.

What About Willow Creek's Seeker-Sensitive Services?

It's hard to discuss worship without mentioning Willow Creek Community Church in South Barrington, Illinois. Admittedly, what Willow Creek has accomplished in reaching the unchurched is amazing. Each weekend more than 15,000 people flock to hear Bill Hybels preach. Is it appropriate to discuss seeker-sensitive worship as practiced at Willow Creek?

Yes and no. Yes, it is wise to know what they're doing and what God is doing through Willow Creek's ministries. Any God-blessed work that has an impact as significant as Willow Creek's deserves at least an informed awareness. But in another sense we can answer no to the question. The reason for not considering Willow Creek's pattern as a main style of worship is that the seeker-sensitive services are not Willow Creek's *worship* services. Willow Creek understands that worship and evangelism are not the same. At this church the Saturday and Sunday seeker-sensitive services are designed to attract and reach secular-minded persons who are separated from organized religion, "unchurched Harry and Mary," as they have been affectionately named. As Robert Webber states,

> I have been greatly impressed that Willow Creek Community Church . . . openly acknowledges that what they do on Sunday morning is not worship. Sunday morning is used for evangelism, for the communication of the gospel through the arts, especially through a creative form of music and drama. . . . Recognizing the need for believer's worship, the church has designated the midweek service . . . as worship. At this time, the committed Christians and members of Willow Creek Community Church gather for believer's worship. The significance of this decision is that a time has been reserved when the church gathers for worship.[21]

What Willow Creek is doing on Sundays is not *seeker-sensitive worship*. What they are doing is better described as *seeker-sensitive evangelism*. To imitate their pattern without understanding this distinction is to ignore a key part of their strategy. One of their most important strategic principles is that you cannot do evangelism and edification optimally at the same time, in the same place, in the same meeting. So to consider a Willow Creek-style service is to lose the focus of worship. Let's not forget that the essential and nonnegotiable work of the Church is to worship God.

Questions to Consider Before Implementing Change

Before we even attempt to make changes in the style of public worship in the church where we lead, we must ask some basic, essential questions. Attempting to implement changes in worship without careful thought invites disaster! Three key issues must be faced when we consider changing worship style. These same issues often remain in continuous tension as we plan, strategize, and even implement changes in worship style. The first question that must be asked is:

What style of worship is the present congregation accustomed to, and how committed are they to that style? The word of advice to heed: *Never underestimate the commitment to tradition.* Remember: worship style is largely a matter of music, and "people especially treasure the music of their formative years, whether the popular music of their youth or the worship patterns of their most formative years spiritually."[22] When even simple changes are thoughtlessly introduced that violate the values of those we seek to lead, we can find more turmoil than we can imagine. We are unwise if we believe that forsaking established tradition is the quick-and-easy way to bring worship renewal to most already established congregations.

A "snapshot" profile of two congregations may provide an instructive look at how change may or may not be accepted. Both congregations are strong churches in the central Midwest, averaging more than 250 in worship.

One church began more than 70 years ago. The church is centrally located in a major city in a mature neighborhood. Many living around the church are retired, having occupied the same houses for 20 or more years. Over the past 25 years this church has had six pastors and one minister of music. In this congregation one could correctly assume that there would be a strong commitment to their own worship patterns. There is great stability in those traditions. If the decision is made to attempt to make significant changes in worship style, it will be essential to work carefully to establish the trust of the congregation, learning their unspoken values and working with key influential leaders if change is to have any chance to succeed.

The second church came into being just 13 years ago. Beginning as a home-mission church and growing rapidly, the congregation knows little except continual change. Adaptation has been necessary from the start. Long-term growth implies continual change. The church is presently located in a rapidly expanding suburban residential neighborhood; the surrounding area is exploding with new housing starts. To this point the congregation has had just one pastor, a founding pastor they dearly love and trust. It should be obvious that in this situation change could more likely happen. Three factors contribute to the probability that change in this congregation could occur more easily: (1) the congregation is experienced at adapting to change; (2) they have a trusted leader who has earned the right to guide them; and (3) the neighborhood around them, their environment, is growing, and thus change seems natural. While it would be wrong to assume there would be no barriers to change, change would probably happen more easily in this second congregation than in the first.

I am convinced that pastors who accept the responsibility to lead established congregations are called by God to shoulder two sometimes conflicting responsibilities. We are first responsible to lead in worship those who have been won to Christ before we came as pastor. We dare not contemptuously abandon the work of our predecessors. We are, for better or worse, a part of a continuing heritage—a heritage that former pastors and worship leaders have laid long before we came. While the congregants may have experienced, learned, and still desire worship styles that are not readily appreciated by our surrounding culture, we still have a responsibility not to abandon them in our desire to reach out to others who don't yet know Jesus. But we are also responsible to find effective and creative ways to take the gospel to the lost. We must continuously call the Church to mission, to reach those who do not yet know Jesus Christ as Lord. These two oft-conflicting responsibilities are carried continuously in tension by the thoughtful worship leader and innovator.

Understanding the dynamics of the situation you lead in worship will enable a better assessment of present worship style and the congregation's commitment to present patterns of worship. But because the worship we lead is for more than just those presently in the church, we face another key question:

What style of worship probably best fits the makeup of your surrounding community or your "target audience"?

- Tim Keller, targeting a cultured population in downtown Manhattan, leads worship services rich in liturgy and classical music.[23]

- Doug Murren developed a style of worship intentionally aimed at baby boomers. "They are drawn to music with a contemporary sound."[24]

- Bill Hybels, in order to reach the secular-minded "Unchurched Harry and Mary," devised a strategy of worship in which "services feature lots of upbeat contemporary music, highly professional singing and clever skits."[25]

None of these pastors leads *your congregation* in *your community!* Don't imitate their style if it doesn't fit the larger dynamics of your situation. Be aware that hundreds of churches have attempted—and failed—to employ the Willow Creek strategy in their setting. Custom-design a worship strategy that fits your place of service. Not only must we consider the congregation we presently serve, but because the mission of the Church of Jesus Christ is evangelistic, we must also consider who our church is called to reach. This will largely be determined by what kinds of people surround us. Not every church will reach every person. We can, however, adjust our worship styles to appeal more to those who surround us. While everyone is welcome, it may be that understanding the surrounding community and its needs will offer essential clues to guide us to design worship services more effectively that can meet the needs of those we are most likely to lead to Jesus Christ.

The third question we must face regards those who will help us:

What talent base in your congregation will supply the musicians, singers, and support personnel to implement your proposed worship style changes?

- A congregation of 1,000 has a talent pool greater than the church of 500.

- A church of 250 deals with a base greater than a church of 100.

- A church of 100 has more resources than a church of 25.

What talent base in your church is available to make envisioned changes possible? Are the people present who can make the new style of service work? Are they willing to commit themselves to work with you in making it happen? It's exciting and perhaps an open door to move ahead when the answer to both these questions is yes!

But in some situations, even where the people are receptive and eager for change, there may not be the talent available to implement those changes. We have to know what assets are available. If, as a pastor-worship leader, all avenues have been explored and still the help needed is unavailable, we may have to be content to do what we can with what we have, where we are—until in God's timing that talent becomes available.

A Closing Observation

Over the past five years I've observed persons worshiping God in differing styles in churches from Los Angeles to Tampa, from Atlanta to Chicago. On America's coasts, as well as in the heartland, I've sensed that God is doing some amazing things in worship. Across the nation, worship is changing dramatically. It's no longer worship as usual. New innovations in some settings, including more contemporary music and the increased use of drama, are being matched by a return to more liturgical patterns in other churches. Both styles are effectively used to lead worshipers to praise God with renewed vigor and excitement. Nothing less than a cross-fertilization is taking place among all styles of worship. Traditional worship seems to be influenced by styles of both a more liturgical and a praise and worship variety.

Robert Webber observes the same phenomena: "Mutual borrowing from the historic and contemporary churches [is resulting in] a convergence of worship traditions. . . . I believe what is happening worldwide in worship is a convergence of the traditions—a convergence that is resulting in the birth of a style of worship that is rooted in the Scriptures, aware of the developments in history, and with a passion for the contemporary."[26]

A case illustrating what God is doing in worship among us is Promise Keepers. Experienced by hundreds of thousands of men across the nation, Promise Keepers brings them together to worship and praise God in a style that transcends the boundaries previously separating us. Through worship, men—young and old, from many denominations—unite as one. It would not have happened 25 years ago. It could not have occurred a decade back. But today God is doing a new thing among us.

7

Expanding Our Vision of Worship

It WAS A MOMENT THAT FIXED ITSELF IN MY MIND for life. On a cool afternoon for a reason I can't remember, my fifth grade teacher, Mrs. Hammill, walked me to the car of my parents, who waited to pick me up after school. I hopped into the backseat as my teacher chatted with Mom and Dad. Then she said it: *"Your son is college material."*

Those five short words changed my life. No one in our family had ever gone to college. I guess you could say our expectations were pretty low. Yet here was a trusted lady who told us that this fifth grade guy could make it in college. With those simple words, the vision for my life expanded dramatically. Looking back, I believe God used Mrs. Hammill to help me envision what might be possible. Before you can, you have to believe you can.

The same applies to worship. Until we expand our vision of what worship can become, we limit what God can do through us. Paul Harvey said that a blind man's world is bounded by the limits of his touch, an ignorant man's world by the limits of his knowledge, and a great man's world by the limits of his vision.[1] At any given time, the boundaries of our vision limit our ability to achieve. Because the size of our vision establishes what we'll attempt, it's essential to expand our worship horizons. This leads us to a critical question: How can we as worship leaders expand our vision of what worship can be?

I'd like to offer several suggestions that may help us see possibilities in worship we have not previously considered. The hope is that God will use our expanded vision to help us lead our people to glorify Him better.

Start with a Genuine Appreciation of the Strengths of Our Present Worship

When we've worked with any group for a while, it's easy to take for granted their strengths and see only their shortcomings. Applying this to worship means that we can come to see mistakenly only where our services are severely lacking. Conversely, we can believe that other churches worship much better than we do—and that can paralyze our vision.

"The Grass Is Always Greener" Syndrome

Not every other church does it better—though sometimes we may think they do. We hear so many success stories that it's easy to believe every other church attracts huge crowds, holds multiple services, and does marvelous, cutting-edge worship—everyone but us. Believing the lie that everyone else worships better can cause us to do dumb things.

Too many worship leaders find themselves chasing the latest fad. "If it works for their church, it should work for us too," the reasoning goes. If the church across town attracts a large crowd when their pastor bungee jumps from the top of the steeple, some are tempted to order the crane and head for the steeple next Sunday—especially if it's the autumn attendance campaign! But worship is too serious to chase fads. Don't cancel choir practice because some success-story church uses a worship team. Don't throw out the hymnal just because Willow Creek flashes praise choruses on a projection screen. Don't think that starting a drama ministry will by itself revolutionize your worship. Don't be so naive as to think that if you just replace your big wooden pulpit with a neat new see-through acrylic one, your services will suddenly be revolutionized. When we chase fads, we end up imitating the wrapping on the package while forgetting it's what's inside that matters.

Identify Strengths in Your Present Worship Patterns

Identifying the strengths in your present services involves answering the question "What do we already do well?" Perhaps you have a good choir, or the musicians are talented and faithful to their ministry. Maybe your service flows well. Perhaps the call to worship is effective, or the services conclude powerfully. Could the way your church handles prayer be especially meaningful to the worshipers? Do the greeters and ushers take their jobs seriously? Maybe a strength of your worship lies in the preaching ministry.

As you consider the strengths of your present worship, remember the people who attend have chosen your services as their place to worship God. Something draws them to worship in this congregation. If the church you lead is large, rejoice that you have a deep talent pool from which to draw. If your church is small, remember that many prefer the family feeling of knowing everyone by name—that's a strength a smaller church offers. Whether it be the warmth and love that flows from the people or a hundred-voice choir, there are strengths in any situation if we will only stop to identify them.

Know Who You Are—Like Who You Are

Besides identifying our strengths, it is also important to have a sense of who we are in worship. The church you lead probably has a story—a way the people describe and think about themselves—that influences how they worship. For example, people in the congregation I presently serve say over and over, "We're a healing congregation." That self-image or story impacts what they perceive to be important in worship. If our services are encouraging and uplifting, if people leave feeling they've been able to lick their wounds and go out to fight their battle one more day, then our folks feel good about the services. The church you lead has a story too.

Once we understand who we are, we decide whether or not we like ourselves. This decision often happens below the level of consciousness. Yet we do decide, consciously or unconsciously, whether to focus on our strengths or on our weaknesses. If we choose to focus on our weaknesses, there will be plenty to fault in any situation. On the other hand, if we choose to focus on our strengths, we can find many positive things to enjoy about our church's worship.

David L. McKenna writes, "In Biblical terms, positive self-regard is recognizing, disciplining, and nurturing our gifts in order to deploy ourselves in servanthood."[2] What a great challenge for us as we consider our worship! We seek greater positive self-understanding in order to develop our gifts and be more effective servants of our Lord Jesus Christ, including worshiping God better.

Appreciating our strengths does not excuse us simply to stay as we are. Appreciating our strengths allows us wisely to avoid destroying all our present worship traditions. It also helps us to make necessary adjustments willingly. With careful modifications, we may polish and add sparkle to our present worship—without engaging in the bloodshed that often accompanies revolutionary change.

Design a Plan to Enlarge Your Own Worship Horizons

Having clearly identified some of our strengths in worship, we come to another important question: How can we, as pastor-worship leaders, expand our worship horizons? There are a couple of things we can do.

We can read. When worship literature is discussed, key names surface. Topping off the list is Robert Webber, who has written a library full of books and articles on worship. His best known is *Worship Is a Verb*. To gain a perspective of the history of worship, look at Webber's *Worship—Old and New* and James F. White's *Protestant Worship: Traditions in Transition*. Among my favorite books on worship is *Mastering Worship*, which is practically oriented and aimed squarely at pastors and worship leaders. The book is written by four prominent experts in worship. Among the featured authors are well-known worship leaders Jack Hayford and also Howard Stevenson, who served as Chuck Swindoll's minister of music. Another prominent name is Duke University's William Willimon. His *Worship as Pastoral Care* calls busy pastors to realize that much pastoral care can be completed through effective leadership in public worship. Willimon's insight is vitally important in a time when many pastors feel pressure to devote huge blocks of time to counseling ministries. He wisely calls us to make leading worship a priority in our ministry.

We can observe worship services in other churches. One of the most beneficial activities I've experienced in trying to broaden my own worship horizons is to visit services in other evangelical Protestant churches that have strong worship programs. No other activity I've experienced has yielded better results more quickly. By seeing what other churches are doing, I've found great help in seeing new possibilities in worship. Over the last four years, I've attended services all across the country as well as in the heart of America, where I live. I've worshiped and watched what's going on. I can hear you respond, "It sounds good, but I'm a pastor, and my congregation strangely expects me to show up on Sunday." I understand. I, too, am expected to lead worship and preach nearly every week. But by careful planning I found I could experience some services I never imagined possible.

If you reside in a city or town where some churches have services at times that differ from your own church's scheduled services, you may be able to squeeze these into your schedule. More and more churches offer early Sunday morning services or Saturday evening worship opportunities. In my case, I explained to the church board my desire to visit several early Sunday morning services over a period of about six weeks. I asked their support in allowing me to arrive at church during the middle of Sunday School for those Sundays. When they understood that they would be the beneficiaries of the ideas I received, they enthusiastically agreed to the plan. If you can find churches in your area that have Saturday evening services, that can work even better. A little planning to fit the service into your schedule is all that's necessary.

Another thing that has been helpful is to use to the fullest the Sundays I'm away from my church. I have attended as many as three worship services on one Sunday. By searching the yellow pages in the cities where I've been, I've almost always been able to find an early service at 8:00 or 8:30 that was close enough to allow me also to attend a 10:45 service elsewhere. Then on Sunday evening I attend one more service. Of course, you or your family may not be quite so enthusiastic. The point remains—if you want to see what's happening in other services, it can be done—even while you're pastoring.

A couple of suggestions may make your visits more productive. First, to make your visits as beneficial as possible, develop a "discerning eye." Learn to look at the services you attend from the perspective of a worshiper. One way I do this is intentionally not announcing that I'm a pastor who is just visiting. I find by coming into the service as "just another visitor," I can more accurately discover what most newcomers to church experience.

Another part of developing a discerning eye is to go to the service having thought through the issues involved in worship. Before I began my visits, I adapted some material from William Willimon's book *Worship as Pastoral Care* to develop a worship service evaluation form. (A sample of the form is included in the Appendix.) Completing these forms at each service I've attended has over time become a valuable resource to enable a fuller and richer appreciation of worship.

Another suggestion is to pick churches whose services will probably stretch you without overwhelming you. This is often a matter of size. As stated earlier, generally the larger the congregation, the larger the resource pool from which it has to draw. I suggest choosing a church that is at least a bit stronger than your accustomed service. Yet, if you lead a church of 25, don't expect to find a lot of help if you choose to visit a church of 2,500. Their immense resources will simply overwhelm and frustrate you.

Understand Some Transitions Necessary to Raise the Level of Congregational Worship

Let's consider some key transitions that will probably need to occur in order to improve the worship in our services.

To raise our level of worship, we'll need to improve the quality of our services. Improving the quality of the service is often a matter of attending to details. Any service is made up of many little parts that fit together to comprise the whole. By giving attention to the individual parts (the details) and how they flow and fit together (the transitions), the quality of the whole service can be lifted.

Obviously we have to keep in mind that worship is a spiritual endeavor aimed at glorifying God. We are not marketing a production. We are organizing ourselves to do the best we can to praise God. Sometimes when persons are challenged to pay more attention to details, they respond saying something like, "That's too much like Hollywood. We're not in the entertainment business at our church." And there's some truth in what they say—we are not in the entertainment industry. However, it's also true that God deserves nothing less than our best effort—which means we attend to the details.

The Old Testament prophet Malachi shows us an amazing disturbance arising in the very heart of God: "'Oh, that one of you would shut the temple doors, so that you would not light useless fires on my altar! I am not pleased with you,' says the LORD Almighty, 'and I will accept no offering from your hands'" (Mal. 1:10).

Why would God consider staging a worship "lockout"? What caused God to desire a shutout of the worshipers? Very plainly we're told—the people came offering God less than their best. Hear God's displeasure: "'When you bring injured, crippled or diseased animals and offer them as sacrifices, should I accept them from your hands?' says the LORD. 'Cursed is the cheat who has an acceptable male in his flock and vows to give it, but then sacrifices a blemished animal to the Lord. For I am a great king,' says the LORD Almighty, 'and my name is to be feared among the nations'" (Mal. 1:13-14).

The whole issue of God's displeasure was over the fact that He was offered less than the best. Since God was upset when these Old Testament worshipers brought Him less than their best, can we believe He will be pleased with us if we come to worship with a halfhearted effort to assemble the elements of the service in a high-quality way?

While I can't prove it, I strongly suspect that the caliber of our services is not nearly as important to God as the quality of our effort. Let me explain. God won't be awed by our worship even if we approach Him with a 200-voice choir, an orchestra, and the best pianists alive. (After all, when we worship we're to stand in awe of Him, not the other way around.) If He chose, God could call together a choir of the heavenly host that would make any of our attempts look pathetic. Even the best of our best won't impress Him. On the other hand, if we come before God with our best effort, I suspect He'll love it even if our singing is feeble, the usher drops the offering plate, and our preaching is mediocre.

Last evening I attended my daughter's piano recital. I sat through only a few numbers before I realized that the students were presented in order of their development. First, beginning students played simple pieces. Then, more-advanced pianists presented songs that were more challenging. At the end of the evening, the most accomplished students presented difficult but well-done pieces. The complexity was handled with grace and style, because they had worked for years to develop their skills.

Sitting near the back, I watched the parents. As their own child went forward to play, parents suddenly got interested. They roused themselves from polite indifference to listen with great attention. It didn't really matter if their child was first (the newest student playing the simplest piece with many "clinkers"), last (the most advanced, technically proficient pianist), or somewhere between (where my daughter, Denise, played a sparkling, tremendous piece—you should have heard her!); when it's your own child, it's great.

If parents of piano students get excited over the best efforts of their own, even if it's not polished perfection, our Heavenly Father can get excited over our efforts too—*if we go to Him with our best.* When we worship, He's more concerned that we do our best than that we "hit all the right notes."

The challenge to do our best applies to everyone: the ushers, the musicians, the singers, the preachers, and those who minister in the background (sound engineers, light technicians, custodians, and so on). If we are to raise the level of our worship, we need to improve the quality of our services.

To raise our level of worship, more opportunities for involvement must be offered. I recently attended a revival service in another church. Just a few folks were present during the midweek service. The song leader led the congregation in praising the Lord and then immediately left the platform. He hustled to the back, where he found offering plates so he could serve as an usher. Finishing that assignment, he hurried to the sound booth to start the accompaniment tape for the special singer just before the sermon. Song leader, usher, sound engineer—obviously they didn't pay him according to how many jobs he did!

Maybe it was a bad night. Probably an usher got sick. Perhaps the sound board operator had an emergency. If we've led worship for long, we've experienced the frustration of people who fail to carry through on their assignments. But the simple truth is that if we are going to raise the quality of the worship in the local church, ways must be found to get more people involved in active ministry. Pew potatoes must be transformed into active participants.

To raise our level of worship, increased attention to planning and coordination is necessary. When more people and groups get involved, more coordination is essential. More participants means more complexity. And more complexity demands more preparation and planning to make all the pieces fit. If, from the perspective of the pew, it looks easy, it probably wasn't. Effectively combining the efforts of greeters, pianists, organists, members of an orchestra, and a choir with those of ushers, sound engineers, light technicians, and maybe a drama team takes great forethought and capable leadership. To raise the level of our worship means we must give more attention to putting all the pieces together.

To raise the level of our worship, our ability to delegate responsibility effectively must grow. Of course, no one can do it all. A key to handling greater and greater complexity is bringing around high-quality people who will share the load. But getting the most out of the people who are available takes a leader who can effectively delegate. John Maxwell offers wisdom for those who want to extend their influence through delegation: "Remember, when you delegate authority to act, you don't abdicate your responsibility to get the job done. If the people to whom you delegate your responsibility fail, the end result is that your leadership has failed. That means you have the right and responsibility to hold people accountable."[3] When we work with volunteers or even paid staff members, setting up the lines of accountability is more easily done when the task is given than after a problem arises.

Asking these 10 questions before delegating a task can help improve our effectiveness in working with others:

1. Exactly what needs to be done?
2. Why does it need to be done?
3. When does it need to be done?
4. Who is the best person to do it?
5. How well must it be done?
6. How much budget is available for getting it done?
7. What training is available for doing this task?
8. What reports do I need from the person who does it?
9. Who else may need to be aware of this assignment?
10. If this isn't done, what difference will it make?[4]

To raise the level of our worship, our ability to delegate responsibility effectively must grow.

To raise our level of our worship, longer planning "lead time" is necessary. I listened as the newly installed pastor of a church of 2,500 shared his vision of altering the worship patterns of the congregation he now served. It wasn't that the present patterns were all bad, but he felt there was room for improvement. I was shocked when he said it would be *at least 18 months* before he could have any real influence. He explained that worship plans were already in place for the next year and a half when he arrived.

Not many of us will have need to work with that much lead time. (Recent statistics tell us that only about 300 out of more than 375,000 churches in the United States have 2,000 or more attenders.[5]) But typically the fact remains that the larger the church, the more people and groups that are involved, and the greater complexity demands more time to coordinate efforts.

In the Florida bay near my mom's home, the windsurfers love to ride their boards. Their "toys" look exciting and fun. The surfboards mounted with sails are quick in the water. Only a little effort is needed to change direction. If the board tips over, it's no big deal—the rider just climbs back on and goes again.

Contrast the wind surfboard with an aircraft carrier. Instead of one, thousands are on board. If the ship tips over, it *is* a very big deal—billions of dollars big! And maneuverability is much decreased on the huge ship. Turning the ship requires not seconds, but minutes, and a wide, wide turn lane. Turning an aircraft carrier is not at all like changing the course of a wind surfboard.

Some worship situations resemble the windsurfer—primarily one-person presentations in which last-second changes are not only possible but normal. Other worship services, greater in size and complexity, are more like the aircraft carrier. A lot of time and effort is required to determine direction and coordinate assignments. Most services are somewhere in between. But the point remains—the greater the complexity, the more time and thought is required to guide a service well. To raise the level of our worship, longer planning lead time is necessary.

A Closing Thought

Until we expand our vision of what worship can become, we limit what God can do. Several years ago *Leadership* told of Apple Computer's struggle. The company desperately needed strong, experienced leadership. The techies that made the company great were ill-equipped to lead the huge corporation that their computer skills had created. Steven Jobs, Apple's young chairman, traveled to New York to recruit PepsiCo's chief executive officer, John Sculley, to assume the helm of Apple.

Sculley was not easy to persuade. He declined Jobs's offer. But then when Jobs persisted, Sculley, thinking he could get rid of him with outrageous demands, laid out what he wanted. His demands included a million-dollar-a-year salary, a million-dollar bonus, and another million guaranteed in severance. To his surprise, Jobs agreed, so long as

Sculley would move to California. But then Sculley would commit only to working as a consultant from New York. It was then that Jobs challenged Sculley: "Do you want to spend the rest of your life selling sugared water, or do you want to change the world?"

Sculley's autobiography, *Odyssey*, reports that the challenge hit home hard. He'd gotten so caught up in protecting his position as head of PepsiCo, preparing his future, and developing his retirement plan, that he nearly let an opportunity to change the world pass him by. Instead, he rethought his priorities and went to work at Apple. A new vision opened the way to new possibilities.[6]

Woodrow Wilson said it: "No man that does not see visions will ever realize any high hope or undertake any high enterprise." A grand and growing vision of worship will allow us to lead His people better to glorify God in the splendor of His holiness.

8

Worship Renewal: Effecting Positive Change in Worship

(or How to Make Worship Changes Without Changing Churches)

SINCE WORSHIP IS THE FOUNTAIN FROM WHICH the life and energy of the church flow, the pastor must take the lead in making worship the best it can be. Continuing to examine and improve the worship offered to God is a responsibility of pastoral leadership. God deserves nothing less than the best we can give. But how can pastors move the church forward in worship? How can we bring our people along with us and not alienate them with the proposed changes? They wisely realize that not all change is progress. Sometimes they resist. Pastors, however, desiring to modify what happens when the church comes together to glorify God, see that there can be no progress unless there is change. How can we effectively guide the church to positive change in worship?

Ten Steps Toward Positive Change

Max De Pree writes, "Leadership is much more an art, a belief, a condition of the heart, than a set of things we do."[1] It can't ever be reduced to "10 quick steps" or "4 easy formulas." Leadership, including pastoral leadership in worship, is complex—less science than craft. As such, no quick-and-simple set of procedures will work in every situation.

In spite of these difficulties involved in reducing leadership to a list of procedures, here are 10 concepts that can help us more effectively lead the congregation we serve through changes in worship. To guide God's people to positive changes in worship—

1. Ask God to provide a clear vision of what needs to change and why. Since worship starts with God, it only makes sense that changes to worship should also originate with Him. God's Word clearly directs us, "If any of you lacks wisdom, he should ask God, who gives generously to all without finding fault, and it will be given to him" (James 1:5). God is interested in guiding us, and He is certainly eager to help us discern what needs to happen in the shaping of public worship.

Richard J. Foster, author of *Celebration of Discipline*, asserts, "To pray is to change. Prayer is the central avenue God uses to transform us. If we are unwilling to change, we will abandon prayer as a noticeable characteristic of our lives."[2] As we who are worship leaders pray, two important issues merit our thought:

God may start the change in us. The saying has been used until it is nearly threadbare: "Prayer changes things." A former college president believed that expression could be improved. "Prayer changes *people*, and *people* change things," he asserted. Perhaps before God shows us what needs to be changed in the worship of our church, He will want to change us! I like Max De Pree's words: "In the end, it is important to remember that we cannot become what we need to be by remaining what we are."[3] God may start the change in us. Unless we are first willing to submit to His shaping, we have no right to ask our people to endure our tinkering with their services. Change begins in us.

The first change necessary in us may be an infusion of courage. Changing worship may not be easy. Far greater support probably exists for keeping things as they are. Few eagerly venture into the unknown. It may take more time and patience to bring about change than we can imagine. It will take courage—God-given courage. A sign on a hospital wall said it well: "Courage is just fear that has said its prayers." We'll need courage to keep going, courage to remain positive, and courage to keep believing in God's people even when they don't eagerly embrace the changes we consider necessary.

Belief in our people is essential. If we ever come to see them as adversaries, we are in great trouble. Rather than adversaries, we must maintain the view that we are teammates—teammates working to accomplish God's work and will. Seeing our folks as fellow workers will guide us through tough times when some dig in their heals in support of the status quo, resisting what we perceive as necessary change. Those opposing change probably aren't really sent our way as the 11th plague—it just seems that way. Acting as agents of change in public worship will take courage, patience, and positive belief. God can give us all we need.

2. Consider the magnitude of change that is needed. Once we clearly understand what needs to happen, we must consider the magnitude of the desired change. Are the desired changes minor, major, or something between? Moving announcements from the middle of the service to before the service is a minor change. Minor changes can happen quickly and with minimal work. On the other hand, adding a second worship service represents a shift of a far greater magnitude—a major change. It is unwise to treat major changes in the same manner as minor ones. As a rule of thumb, remember that the greater the magnitude of change required, the more carefully the change process needs to be managed.

Managing change includes providing clear and accurate information so there are no surprises. We manage change by allowing time for people to warm to an idea, to come to own it for themselves. If possible, we want them even to come to feel it was their idea in the beginning. John Naisbitt advises, "People whose lives are affected by a decision must be part of the process of arriving at that decision."[4] We manage change by guiding folks through the necessary adjustments, encouraging them to see the value and future benefits of adapting to new habits and patterns. We manage change as we help them see how the changes improve our worship of God. We manage change by showing sensitivity to negative feedback.

For example, as we talked with our congregation about starting a second Sunday morning worship service designed to reach more effectively those who may not have long-term church backgrounds, we found there was serious concern over the proposed "contemporary" service. "What is this crazy pastor trying to do?" seemed to be the question of some. "Is he wanting to introduce rock music into our services?" Very early on, we discovered that the word "contemporary" meant so many differing things that it was to our advantage to stop calling our proposed new service "contemporary." When we began to discuss instead our new "early service," we found the opposition was diffused, and the process proceeded smoothly.

Sensitivity to the connotations associated in the minds of some with the word "contemporary" was an important change-management factor. To guide the congregation effectively through changes in worship, consider the magnitude of the necessary changes, and create a plan to manage the issues involved.

3. Earn the trust of your people. Since nothing is more public than the pastor's leading of corporate worship, establishing trust as an effective worship leader will make other changes possible. If the congregation comes to feel comfortable with the regular services of worship, they will more easily believe that proposed changes suggested by their trusted leader will be good ones. If people can feel good about what they already see, they will probably find it easier to be supportive of what they have not yet experienced.

It is important that the worship leader work within the boundaries of the people's trust. To bring about positive, lasting change that results in God's glorification and the people being drawn closer to Him, working within the boundaries of trust is necessary. Most churches will follow wise leadership in worship if change is carefully implemented within such boundaries. Knowing the boundaries means knowing the people. Some churches have broad, flexible boundaries. Others have much narrower constraints. When we understand that genuine worship is an act of the people, not just the preference or desire of the pastor-worship leader, then we can see that the leader must not transgress the boundaries of the people's trust. It is within the community of faith that corporate worship is conducted, and it is within these boundaries of the trust of the community that change is effectively implemented.

How do we earn trust? What can we do to build the confidence of the people we seek to lead? Three areas deserve mention.

We establish trust in worship by having good worship services. Perhaps the two most obvious and important components of good worship services are music and preaching. A service with good music and good preaching will have a good chance of being a good service! Of the two, many pastors will find preaching easier to control. While not all of us are master pulpiteers, we can come to the pulpit fully prepared and ready to proclaim the gospel. While all preachers probably envy those with extraordinary preaching skills, the truth remains that the most significant factor in good preaching is not natural skill but hard work. Our people know when we come prepared. They sense when we take preaching seriously. They know when they are being fed a nourishing spiritual meal. They also discern when they are offered spiritual "fast food."

139

While good preaching is probably easier for pastor-worship leaders to control, we can't minimize the importance of the music. While the size of the congregation and more specifically the size of its talent base will largely determine the quality and capabilities of the music in the services, it is essential that we get the best of what is available.

Early in my ministry I focused almost entirely on the preaching ministry, believing that it was good preaching that would cause the congregation to move forward. The longer I lead services of worship, the more I realize that many people form their opinions on a church more on the quality of the music than on the quality of the preaching. The synergistic insight in the observation "Music opens the heart—the Word fills it" rightly says both are important. We establish trust with our people by having good worship services.

We establish trust in worship by building strong relationships. Competence and consistency are essential elements in building trust. But one cannot expect to build a base of trust apart from realizing that all ministry, including leadership in worship, is relational. If people like you, you can do little wrong. Conversely, if people don't like you, it will be hard to do anything right.

A study was done in the business world that examined the relative importance between product knowledge and skill in getting along with people. The study found that success in business was built only 12.5 percent on product knowledge but 87.5 percent on the ability to get along with people. While the Church is not the business world, the dynamics of effective leadership still depend on our ability to work with others. People more willingly follow those they like. Lyle Schaller wisely advises, "Relational leaders intuitively know that the primary level of trust is personal. Friends and acquaintances listen more openly to proposals for change than do strangers."[5]

We establish trust in worship by showing sensitivity to the values of our people. By showing that we're sensitive to the issues and values of the people we lead, we make it possible for them to relax. They can follow believing that their concerns and values will not be trampled. Increased openness to change is an obvious benefit. While leaders won't hold every value espoused as their own, it is important to be aware of those values that are held by many of the people. Remember: not every battle is worth fighting. Sometimes we win by choosing which battles we don't fight. We build trust more quickly by focusing on those issues that unite us rather than by quibbling over minor issues on which we disagree.

4. Understand the key role of influence leaders. To lead a congregation effectively through change does not mean that 100 percent of the people must agree with the proposed changes. However, if proposed change is to be adopted, it is a great help if the key influence leaders are supportive, or at least not in opposition, to the concept. Key influence leaders carry more than their single vote. Others look to influence leaders to see how they should respond. To gain the support of an influence leader is to gain the support of those they influence. A wise pastor knows who the influence leaders are and works to build solid relationships with them.

5. Examine the worship dynamics in your situation. Answering three key questions will provide increased understanding of the worship dynamics in the congregation you lead.

How deep is the talent well from which you draw? Generally, the size of the congregation determines the depth of the talent well. In a large congregation there may be plenty of folks available to provide strong music leadership. In a small church it may be a luxury to have a good pianist and song leader. A large congregation will be able to provide the talent to support a traditional service as well, one focusing on a more contemporary style. The smaller church does not have those options available. The depth of the talent well influences what can and cannot be done in worship.

In addition to musical talent, many churches are now discovering the benefits of drama. Short skits, sometimes involving only two to four participants and few props, support the service's theme and make it possible to communicate dramatically messages that could seem harsh if said in the sermon. When used effectively, drama has the advantage of catching people with their defenses down. Whether drama is used will frequently depend, at least in part, on the depth of the talent well. A key issue is the availability of personnel to staff the worship functions. A second question enabling us more realistically to appraise the worship dynamics in our place of service is:

What are the musical preferences of the people in the pews? In understanding the worship dynamics of a local congregation, the musical preferences of the people must be considered. My first two positions on church staff provided a fascinating contrast in musical style. The first congregation in which I served preferred anthems and classical arrangements. It was definitely a people with highbrow musical tastes. A significant culture shock—about 8.0 on the Richter scale, I would judge—occurred when I took my next assignment and discovered the congregation described themselves as hillbillies. Three electric guitars accompanied every chorus, hymn, or gospel song the congregation sang.

In retrospect, the stark differences between the two congregations are amusing. These two groups of people, who both loved their Lord, taught me that the musical preferences of the people must be considered. Understanding the local worship dynamics requires that we know our people's preferences.

How flexible or rigid are attitudes about the way worship should be done? Some congregations change constantly. The only thing that remains constant for these groups is change. More stable churches come to take pride in their never-changing worship patterns. Certain churches value spontaneity and see differing patterns of worship positively. Others value stability and see change as threatening. Before an attempt to shape the worship of any congregation is launched, the pastor would be wise to know how flexible or rigid attitudes are toward worship.

6. Don't underestimate the power of tradition.

"All my fathers have been churchmen 1,900 years or so.
And to every new suggestion they have always answered, 'No!'"[6]

In many congregations, tradition is a powerful force. Precedent often directs future patterns and thinking. Preferred worship patterns develop over the course of decades. They probably won't shift in the course of weeks. Tradition is a formidable force. But tradition is not necessarily bad. While it can be negatively perceived, positive aspects of tradition exist.

Tradition provides stability. Past worship patterns heavily influence present worship forms and preferences. This is to be expected. Patterns used in previous services provide worshipers and worship leaders with a guide that enables them to worship God more effectively. Tradition allows the people to forget the forms and patterns of worship and to be more caught up in glorifying God.

H. Ray Dunning says tradition is one way God is revealed. The word "tradition," he says, "is derived from the Latin word *traditio*, signifying that which is passed on." Dunning reminds us of our debt to those who have faithfully passed to us the revelation of God through lasting traditions, including, I suppose, certain inherited patterns of worship. He also reminds us of the obligation to deliver faithfully to others that uncompromised revelation.[7] Tradition provides stability that allows God to reveal himself to generation after generation. But tradition has a negative side too.

Tradition can cause stagnation. It is possible that some worship traditions could actually hinder an effective gospel presentation to contemporary culture. While society is rapidly changing, churches can be hesitant or slow to change. Those who know typical tendencies of churches realize that the plea "But we've never done it that way before" is an almost instinctive response to proposed change. This is especially true in worship. Worship patterns to which the people become accustomed become comfortable and take on a sense of "rightness" that strongly resists change. Howard Stevenson observes, "People especially treasure the music of their formative years, whether the popular music of their youth or the worship patterns of their most formative years spiritually. It's these experiences of the sacred that indelibly stamp themselves on people's minds and create worship memories that we tamper with at our peril."[8]

But when worship leaders do not gradually modify patterns of worship, stability can breed stagnation. If we are not cautious, we can quit asking the question "What patterns of worship will most effectively present God to the people?" Instead, we may unconsciously substitute the question "How do I prefer to worship?" or "To what are we accustomed?" Outreach is thwarted and mission sacrificed on the altar of maintenance. Just as a stream that ceases to flow eventually stagnates, so, too, a worship tradition that ceases to evolve loses its vitality and winsomeness. Tradition must remain the servant of God and the Church. When tradition ceases to serve the interests of the Lord, it becomes god, and that is idolatrous. While tradition deserves respect, it does not merit worship. However, as worship change agents, we must not underestimate the power of tradition.

7. Start early—be patient. While clear vision is important, patience and persistence are also necessary. If the anticipated changes in services of worship are truly worthwhile, they will still be important six months, a year, or five years from now. It is unwise to force changes in worship before the congregation can readily accept them. Proper timing is essential. But waiting for the right time demands patience. An impatient and hurried implementation of changes in worship will often elicit resistance. Careful, consistent, and persistent forward progress will usually have far greater long-term positive impact. Through patiently moving ahead, the envisioned changes can become reality.

8. Build momentum. When morale is high, attendance is increasing, and giving is up, check the obituaries—you may already be in heaven! If you find yourself still responsible for leading an earthly congregation in worship, realize that momentum makes changes easier to implement. Excitement makes a great difference. It is easy to change the direction of a moving car. It is hard to steer a parked one. Likewise, changes become easier to implement when you can ride the forward flow of momentum.

9. If possible, change only one thing at a time—move forward incrementally. Rapid change characterizes our time. Before we can absorb the changes that are already upon us, more variations force their way into our lives. Church is a place where people long to feel a sense of stability and security. For many, the Church represents an island of dependability in a sea of uncertainty. This fact points us to the importance of not forcing changes in worship too rapidly. If change can be introduced incrementally, we permit our people to adopt the initial changes before more are thrust upon them. By introducing change incrementally, we will find several relatively insignificant changes can add up to a great deal of change without the people experiencing shock. Abe Lincoln's words show great wisdom: "I walk slowly, but I never walk backward."

With a clearly conceived idea of how worship in the congregation should be shaped, incremental steps can lead to long-range forward movement. The guiding vision permits incremental changes that move forward toward the goal of more effective worship services.

10. Work for long-term positive change. In the long-term plan to shape services of Christian worship, the journey is at least as important as the destination. Starting where the people are is the journey's beginning. And since God's worship is the work of the people (not just the performance of the pastor-worship leader), taking our people with us on the journey is the sole option. Our goal is to build up persons and to lead them closer to Christ Jesus, not to alienate them from us and possibly Him by forcing change upon them.

The prophet Amos asks, "Do two walk together unless they have agreed to do so?" (Amos 3:3). The obvious answer is matched by the realization that neither does a congregation follow the pastor's leadership in worship unless they agree on styles, patterns, and forms. But the journey's beginning is not its end. The wise worship leader carefully and conscientiously shapes the services of worship in a manner that encourages progress together in responsible and effective worship of God.

APPENDIX

Worship Service Evaluation Form

(This form is adapted from William Willimon's book *Worship as Pastoral Care*, 64ff. Copyright © 1979 by Abingdon Press. Used by permission.)

Church: _____

Date and Time: _____

General Comments: _____

_____

_____

_____

Some Key Questions

1. **What were my initial impressions on entering the church building?** How was I received? What follow-up structures were used to continue contact with me?

2. **Awareness of the holy.** What appears sacred to them?

3. **Providence.** What does this church's worship life say about their views of the nature of God's purpose toward them?

4. **Faith.** Where are this church's commitments?

5. **Grace.** To what extent and in what ways is the grace of God evident in the services?

6. **Repentance.** In what ways does the service encourage a turning to the better, a positive change toward God?

7. **Communion and Community.** How does the worship experience bring the worshiper into oneness with other worshipers?

8. **Vocation.** What is the group's sense of purpose? How is this communicated?

Some General Observations

9. What style of music was used? (Hymns? gospel songs? choruses?)

10. What was the average age and socioeconomic makeup of the congregation?

11. What does the setting of the service say about this church's worship of God?

12. In what ways are persons encouraged to be actively involved in the service?

13. Was the worship service primarily God-centered or person-oriented? How?

14. What was the impact of the service upon me?

15. What worship strengths were evident in this service?

16. What worship weaknesses were evident in this service?

17. How did this service appeal to the
   a. mind?

   b. emotions?

   c. will?

18. Are there changes that I would like to see in our worship services as a result of my visit in this service?

NOTES

Chapter 1

1. Robert E. Webber, *Worship Is a Verb* (Nashville: Abbott-Martyn, 1992), 7-8.

2. Ibid., 203-4.

3. Anne Ortlund, *Up with Worship* (Ventura, Calif.: Regal Books, 1982), 35-36.

4. William M. Greathouse, "The Present Crisis in Our Worship," *Preacher's Magazine*, December-January-February 1989-90, 4.

5. Ibid., 5.

6. Ibid.

7. James R. Spruce, *Come, Let Us Worship* (Kansas City: Beacon Hill Press of Kansas City, 1986), 52-53.

8. Dennis J. Crocker, "Music and Worship," *Preacher's Magazine*, December-January-February 1989-90, 11.

9. James F. White, *Protestant Worship: Traditions in Transition* (Louisville, Ky.: Westminster/John Knox Press, 1989), 174.

10. Robert Webber, *Worship: Old and New* (Grand Rapids: Zondervan Publishing House, 1982), 83.

11. Quoted in Spruce, *Come, Let Us Worship*, 10.

12. Second Corinthians 8—9 provides a rich foundation for understanding biblical principles of giving.

13. Ortlund, *Up with Worship*, 34.

14. William Greathouse, "The State of the Church," *Ministers' Tape Club* (Kansas City: Beacon Hill Press of Kansas City, April 1984), audiocassette.

15. *International Standard Bible Encyclopedia*, rev. ed. (1979-88), ed. Geoffrey W. Bromiley (Grand Rapids: William B. Eerdmans Publishing Co., 1988), s.v. "Worship," by Ralph P. Martin.

16. Thomas Oden, *Pastoral Theology: Essentials of Ministry* (San Francisco: Harper and Row, 1983), 86.

17. Ibid., 91.

18. Ibid., 90.

Chapter 2

1. Oden, *Pastoral Theology*, 99.

2. William H. Willimon, *Worship as Pastoral Care* (Nashville: Abingdon Press, 1990), 96-99.

3. Greathouse, "The Present Crisis in Our Worship," 6.

4. Robert Macy, Associated Press, January 19, 1982.

5. Greathouse, "The State of the Church."

6. Oden, *Pastoral Theology*, 102.

7. H. Ray Dunning, *Grace, Faith, and Holiness* (Kansas City: Beacon Hill Press of Kansas City, 1988), 187-88.

8. Webber, *Worship Is a Verb*, 91.

9. R. B. Y. Scott, "The Book of Isaiah, Chapters 1—39; Introduction and Exegesis," in *The Interpreter's Bible* (Nashville: Abingdon Press, 1952-57), 5:154.

10. Webber, *Worship Is a Verb*, 30.

11. Greathouse, "The Present Crisis in Our Worship," 29.

12. David Seamands, *Healing of Memories* (Wheaton, Ill.: Victor Books, 1985), 72.

13. Ralph H. Alexander, "847 (*yada*)," in *Theological Wordbook of the Old Testament*, ed. R. Laird Harris et al. (Chicago: Moody Press, 1980), 2:364.

14. Webber, *Worship Is a Verb*, 47.

15. John Wesley, *Sunday Service of the Methodists in North America*, Methodists Bicentennial Commemorative Reprint (Nashville: United Methodist Publishing House and United Methodist Board of Higher Education, 1984), 125.

16. John Wesley, "A Plain Account of Christian Perfection," in *The Works of John Wesley*, 3rd ed. (Kansas City: Beacon Hill Press of Kansas City, 1978), 11:396.

17. William Barclay, *The Beatitudes and Lord's Prayer for Everyman* (New York: Harper and Row, 1963), 34-35.

18. Oden, *Pastoral Theology*, 101.

19. Quoted in Greathouse, "The State of the Church," emphasis added.

20. Quoted by Franklin Segler, *Christian Worship: Its Theology and Practice* (Nashville: Broadman Press, 1967), 90.

21. Webber, *Worship: Old and New,* 25.

22. Quoted in Howard Stevenson, "Creative Music and Worship," *Your Church,* winter 1993, 3W.

Chapter 3

1. Jack Hayford, *Mastering Worship* (Portland, Oreg.: Multnomah Books, 1991), 125.

2. Webber, *Worship Is a Verb,* 212.

3. Ibid., 213.

4. George C. Hunter, *How to Reach Secular People* (Nashville: Abingdon Press, 1992), 153.

5. Ibid., 165.

6. Ibid., 165-66.

7. Webber, *Worship Is a Verb,* 212.

8. Lyle Schaller, *Strategies for Change* (Nashville: Abingdon Press, 1993), 103.

Chapter 4

1. Hayford, *Mastering Worship,* 20-21.

2. Heard on one of Swindoll's radio broadcasts.

3. D. W. Hildie, "Better than Gimmicks," *Preacher's Magazine,* June-July-August 1988, 25.

4. This dramatic reading occurred at Pasadena (California) First Church of the Nazarene in a service led by its pastor, Stephen Green.

5. George Barna, *What Americans Believe* (Ventura, Calif.: Regal Books, 1991), 291.

6. Webber, *Worship: Old and New,* 123.

7. Wesley Tracy, "What They Are Saying About Our Preaching," *Preacher's Magazine,* September-October-November 1992, 30-34.

8. Ibid., 33.

9. Ibid., 34.

10. Ibid.

11. Oden, *Pastoral Theology*, 127.

12. David Buttrick, *Homiletic* (Philadelphia: Fortress, 1988), 225.

13. The terms "Teflon church" and "Velcro church" were borrowed from fall 1990 *Leadership* journal articles.

14. Calvin C. Ratz, "The Velcro Church," *Leadership*, fall 1990, 43.

Chapter 5

1. David Hesselgrave, ed., *Theology and Mission* (Grand Rapids: Baker Book House, 1978), 330.

2. Leith Anderson, *Dying for Change* (Minneapolis: Bethany House, 1990), 43.

3. Robert Bellah et al., eds., *Uncivil Religion: Interreligious Hostility in America* (New York: Crossroad, 1986), 229.

4. George Gallup and Jim Castelli, *The People's Religion: American Faith in the 90s* (New York: Macmillan, 1989), 252.

5. William Irwin Thompson as quoted in Richard L. Rapson, *American Yearnings: Love, Money, and Endless Possibility* (Lanham, Md.: University Press of America, 1988), 140.

6. Gallup and Castelli, *The People's Religion*, 90.

7. Bellah et al., *Habits of the Heart*, 23.

8. CBS Television News special report, April 18, 1995.

9. Gallup and Castelli, *The People's Religion*, 69.

10. Ibid., 70.

11. Ron Blue's comments aired on James Dobson's radio program "Focus on the Family," January 16, 1990.

12. Peter L. Berger, *The Noise of Solemn Assemblies* (Garden City, N.Y.: Doubleday and Co., 1961), 43.

13. Anderson, *Dying for a Change*, 37.

14. Bellah et al., *Habits of the Heart*, 285.

15. Ibid., 284.

16. James W. Fowler, *The Stages of Faith* (New York: Harper and Row, 1981), 4.

17. Andrew Stern, Reuters News Service, April 13, 1995.

18. Allan Bloom, *The Closing of the American Mind* (New York: Simon and Schuster, 1987), 25-26.

19. Bellah et al., *Habits of the Heart*, 6.

20. Anderson, *Dying for a Change*, 89.

21. Ibid., 32.

22. John R. Stott, *Down to Earth: Studies in Christianity and Culture* (Grand Rapids: William B. Eerdmans Publishing Co., 1980), 338.

23. Kenneth Bedell and Alice M. Jones, eds., *Yearbook of American and Canadian Churches 1992* (Nashville: Abingdon Press, 1992), 34.

24. Gallup and Castelli, *The People's Religion*, 46.

25. Lee Stroebel, *Inside the Mind of Unchurched Harry and Mary* (Grand Rapids: Zondervan Publishing House, 1993), 77.

26. Gallup and Castelli, *The People's Religion*, 44.

27. Anderson, *Dying for Change*, 87.

28. Walter Pincus, "Spy Rationalized Betrayal to Country, Comrades," *Los Angeles Times/Washington Post* Service, April 29, 1994.

29. Berger, *The Noise of Solemn Assemblies*, 38.

30. Bellah et al., *Habits of the Heart*, 224.

31. Gallup and Castelli, *The People's Religion*, 253.

32. Bellah et al., *Habits of the Heart*, 78.

33. Rapson, *American Yearnings*, 181.

Chapter 6

1. "In the Name of God," broadcast on ABC television news, March 16, 1995.

2. Elmer Towns, *Ten of Today's Most Innovative Churches* (Ventura, Calif.: Regal Books, 1990), 195.

3. Ibid., 197.

4. Ibid., 193.

5. Ibid., 197.

6. Leith Anderson, *Dying for Change*, 32.

7. Doug Murren, *The Baby Boomerang* (Ventura, Calif.: Regal Books, 1990), 35.

8. Webber, *Worship Is a Verb*, 129.

9. Quoted by Hunter, *How to Reach Secular People*, 151.

10. Robert Webber, *The Worship Phenomena* (Nashville: Abbott-Martyn, 1994), 80.

11. White, *Protestant Worship*, 23.

12. John Killenger, *Mastering Worship* (Portland, Oreg.: Multnomah Books, 1991), 114-15.

13. White, *Protestant Worship*, 198.

14. Webber, *The Worship Phenomena*, 54.

15. Ibid., 92.

16. White, *Protestant Worship*, 197.

17. Ibid., 171.

18. Ibid., 172.

19. Ibid., 171.

20. Webber, *The Worship Phenomena*, 49.

21. Ibid., 61.

22. Stevenson, "Creative Music and Worship," 3W.

23. "What It Takes to Worship Well," *Leadership*, spring 1994, 17ff.

24. Murren, *The Baby Boomerang*, 188-89.

25. Tom Valeo, "Why Do 12,000 People a Week Flock to Hear What This Man Has to Say?" *Arlington Heights, Illinois, Daily Herald*, May 18, 1988, 2.

26. Webber, *The Worship Phenomena*, ix-x.

Chapter 7

1. John Maxwell, *Developing the Leader Within You* (Nashville: Thomas Nelson Publishers, 1993), 138.

2. David L. McKenna, *Renewing Our Ministry* (Waco, Tex.: Word Books, 1986), 43.

3. John Maxwell, "Don't Dump . . . Delegate," *Injoy Life Club* (El Cajon, Calif.: Injoy, 1991), audiocassette 7:5.

4. Bobb Biehl, quoted by John Maxwell in "The Delights of Delegation," *Injoy Life Club* (El Cajon, Calif.: Injoy, 1989), audiocassette 4:7.

5. Leith Anderson, *Winning the Values War in a Changing Culture*, as quoted in "To Verify . . . Statistics for Christian Communication," *Leadership*, spring 1995, 70.

6. Greg Asimakoupoulos, "Vision," *Leadership*, spring 1991, 44.

Chapter 8

1. Max De Pree, *Leadership Is an Art* (New York: Doubleday, 1989), 136.

2. Richard J. Foster, *Celebration of Discipline* (New York: Harper and Row, 1978), 30.

3. De Pree, *Leadership Is an Art*, 87.

4. John Naisbitt, *Megatrends* (New York: Warner Books, 1982), 159.

5. Lyle Schaller, *Strategies for Change* (Nashville: Abingdon Press, 1993), 101.

6. Quoted by James Spruce, "Worship and Preaching Helps," June-July-August 1987.

7. Dunning, *Grace, Faith, and Holiness*, 77-78.

8. Howard Stevenson, "Creative Music and Worship," 4W.

	DATE DUE		